Shaykh Fadhlalla Haeri t
Holy City of Karbala, Iraq i
the United States. His p i
the founding of compan l
as in international business. The rediscovery of the full
Islamic heritage of his birth and its prophetic perfection
came about through an awakening to the inner meanings
of its outer teachings and practices.

Since the 1970s, Shaykh Haeri has given discourses
and taught extensively throughout his travels, both in the
East and the West. He currently resides in England and
continues to travel and lecture widely, and is the author
of many books.

The *Elements Of* is a series designed to present high quality introductions to a broad range of essential subjects.

The books are commissioned specifically from experts in their fields. They provide readable and often unique views of the various topics covered, and are therefore of interest both to those who have some knowledge of the subject, as well as those who are approaching it for the first time.

Many of these concise yet comprehensive books have practical suggestions and exercises which allow personal experience as well as theoretical understanding, and offer a valuable source of information on many important themes.

THE ELEMENTS OF
ISLAM

Shaykh Fadhlalla Haeri

ELEMENT

Shaftesbury, Dorset • Rockport, Massachusetts
Brisbane, Queensland

CONTENTS

ACKNOWLEDGEMENTS

Zainab Hussain Haeri has been an invaluable help in the writing of this book. Without her discipline, perseverance, loyalty and hard work this book would not have been produced. Special thanks are also due to Muna Bilgrami for her superb editing, and to Dr Ya'qub Zaki for his valuable comments and corrections on the history section.

Encouragement and help also came from many friends and well-wishers. I offer my thanks to them all.

FOREWORD

Human beings are the veil of God, and Muslims are the veil of Islam. This book tries to lift the veil without prejudice, condemnation or bitterness.

Islam – submission – is easy. Witnessing and affirming that there is only One God is a reality accessible to everyone. This truth is encapsulated in the first phrase of the Muslim creed: 'I witness that there is no god but God.' The translation of the complementary second half of this testimony of belief, that 'Muhammad is the Messenger of Allah', is harder to decode. This is because through time its misapplication has clouded over its transformational dynamism.

The reader is strongly urged to read this book more than once and with patience, for not until he or she has imbibed all the tessellating parts touched upon in this brief introduction to the reality of Islam will it be possible to break through the distraction of form to arrive at the transformation of meaning.

INTRODUCTION

Surely the [true] religion with Allah is Islam.

Qur'an 3:19

The purpose of this book is to provide a brief, simple and factual account of Islam and Muslims at a time when cultural, racial, religious and other prejudices are prevalent throughout the world. Many of these prejudices, suspicions and fears are disguised behind subtle and civilized veneers; but in a world that is shrinking because of easy communication and travel, bridges between the people of Islam and those who are suspicious or fearful of it must be built.

If we look at the events of the recent past, we notice that since the Islamic revolution in Iran, and the dismantling of Communism, the world has been heading towards greater confrontation between Muslim and non-Muslim culture. I hope this book will cut through what is at present a morass of misunderstanding, misinformation and confrontation so as to reach a deeper and truer understanding. Better understanding can only benefit mankind and lead to greater harmony.

This book gives an overview of the origin, meaning and universality of the prophetic message of Islam. In order to understand Islam, however, one must also understand something of the history of the Muslim peoples. Unless a clear distinction is made between original Islam and the behaviour of Muslims, the current confusion could become magnified into greater and more dangerous controversy and

1

confrontation. A necessarily brief history is therefore also outlined.

Islam is the culmination of all the faiths emanating from the Fertile Crescent. The prophetically revealed knowledge connected all aspects of life, the material and the metaphysical. Though the advent of the Muhammadi message (that is, the revelation of the Qur'an through Muhammad) was the seal of all previous prophetic messages, it was not the beginning of Islam. Islam – that transactional state of joyful surrender to Allah – had been prescribed from the dawn of humankind, symbolized by the entry of Adam into the world of duality.

The rapid spread of Islam and its subsequent power and acceptance by hundreds of nations and millions of people from the extreme north-east of Asia to all of Africa and to parts of Europe, is a phenomenon that has often defied objective analysis and understanding but which proves that people have been and still are prepared to hear the final Islamic reminder. That viability remains a factor in our present world, where so-called rational and materialist/structuralist approaches are unable to bridge the widening gaps and conflicts within the human race.

During the past few years a plethora of books on Islam has appeared in the supermarkets of mass communication in the West. Many of these have been written to make sense of current affairs and the acceleration of events that are increasingly bringing Islam and the behaviour of Muslims into the media spotlight.

Most Western writers on Islam and Muslims are alien to the path of Islam. They have not experienced its transformative element and as a result most of their writings remain somewhat academic and remote, often hailing from an inherent (and therefore unquestioned) attitude of superiority. If a writer is alien to the Islamic transformative process then it follows that most of his observations and commentary on Islam or on Muslim behaviour and culture will be generally superficial despite appearing to reflect depth in their analysis. For example, in discussing the Qur'an, there is an unmistakable difference between trying to understand it, absorb it and be transformed by it, and reviewing it in the same way as any other book might be critically appraised. The Qur'an was never a book but a revelation. It is the inscribed 'tablet' that connects the physical worlds with that of the unseen and the divine dimension beyond time and space.

The Qur'an and the prophetic teachings transcend structuralist approaches for they are based on faith, trust and transformation wrought by following the path of submission. In studying Islam and Muslims the orientalists and others representing European interests have been motivated by academic, practical, material, political or economic aims. They have therefore concentrated on cultural and behavioral patterns, focusing on the differences between Muslim peoples, rather than on the unifying foundation that is Islam.

The first chapter of this book is essentially an introductory overview. I have tried to follow the chronology of the Byzantine and Sassanian Empires and to fill in a brief background on Arab tribalism and the model of life in Medina in order to enable the reader to move forward into an understanding of the history of Muslims.

Before starting on the history and development of the religion, however, it is necessary to give a brief introduction to what the unific path of Islam is and what it encompasses. In the second chapter, therefore, I have tried to show the basic foundation and purpose of creation. Using the Islamic teaching of the Qur'an and the prophetic way of Muhammad, we find the total interconnection between knowledge of the self and the human metaphysical dilemma of life, death and the purpose of existence totally mirrored in the world at large.

Chapter 3 describes the creed of Islam, its ritual practices, its outer bounds and laws, as well as the related commandments. It was these that subsequently came to be called the Pillars of the Faith. How the fundamental, pristine and simple teachings of the Qur'an and the Prophet developed into a full theological and legalistic jurisprudence that was codified in numerous schools of thought is outlined in the fourth chapter.

Though the fifth chapter on the history of the Muslims is comparatively longer than the others it is very condensed. I have attempted to cover a broad and complex subject in a simplified and abbreviated fashion in order to show how the behaviour of Muslims naturally reflected changes from age to age and also occasionally deviated from the original Islamic code of conduct. This information provides a necessary, if turgid, historical backdrop without which it would be impossible to understand the Muslim world today.

In Chapter 6 I have tried to illustrate some aspects of Muslim cultural, social and economic life. I have consciously avoided dwelling on the great artistic, scientific and scholastic contributions Muslims have made to global culture because such information is easily available. I have however touched on a few points that may help to answer some questions (and raise more) that arise out of current events concerning Muslims.

The epilogue highlights certain factors and important points which need to be borne in mind if we are to move into a future where the relationship between Muslim and non-Muslim is to improve, and where there is improved cross-fertilization between Western cultures and the rising tide of Islam.

1 · THE RISE OF ISLAM

It is said that there are as many ways to God as there are human beings. From the rise of human consciousness in the creation of Adam there have been people who have transcended the normal levels of consciousness. These people were the great men of wisdom in the Far East, the Rishis of India and the Prophets and Messengers of the Middle East, Egypt and elsewhere.

It is a natural part of human life to seek the answers to the questions of existence, the meaning behind all change and experience in this life, the meaning of death and what lies beyond. As far back as nine thousand years ago before history came to be recorded, and even before man settled down into agricultural communities, metaphysical insights were already being codified and institutionalized into religions in many parts of the world, especially in the Middle East. Once the immediate physical needs of man have been satisfied, the question arises as to what lies beyond the visible world. This question is the basis of the quest for God or, to put it another way, for the very source and essence of creation.

Whenever we accept a situation, we are submitting and connecting our system of knowledge to the knowledge of that particular situation. When we come to understand a reality of physical nature, that very understanding contains a submission to that reality. Similarly, as we learn to understand our own nature, we submit to that understanding, until a time comes when we can survey the entire vista of understanding through total submission. The rise of Islam is therefore equated with the rise of Adam, for all the Prophets and Messengers arrived at their knowledge through submission to Reality, which is Islam – submission to the will of God. All Prophets and Messengers therefore, were transformed through Islam.

Islam as realized in time relates to the completion of this awakening. The path of transacting in order to maintain and experience the totality of the knowledge that is Islam was crystallized with the Seal of the Prophets and Messengers some fourteen hundred years ago, through the agency of the last great Prophet, Muhammad. By the 'Seal of Prophets' we recognize the completion of the prophetic teachings and paths that had been appearing in numerous waves for thousands of years before. His prophethood represents the completion of the universality of the prophetic light and knowledge. While Adam and all the Prophets were Prophets of Islam, from Muhammad's time onwards anyone could have access to that complete system for awakening to the highest spiritual state without superstition or cultural veils of habit.

Although the final historical Islamic phenomenon occurred some fourteen hundred years ago, Islam actually arose with the awakening of the Adamic consciousness to the meaning of life, death, the return journey and other facets of the unseen. While Adam and all the Prophets were Prophets of Islam, the collective prophetic consciousness reached its completion with Muhammad (whose name means 'most praiseworthy' or 'admirable').

The Qur'an says: 'We make no distinction between any of the Messengers and Prophets [i.e. in the eyes of God]' (3:84). All the Prophets of Islam shared between them the knowledge of God but advocated different outer rules and regulations for the well-being of human transaction in society. The optimum outer bounds and basic laws of conduct were thus universalized for all human beings and for all time by the last of the Prophets, Muhammad.

The rise of Islam in the revelation of the Qur'an and the prophetic conduct (called Sunnah) superseded all previously revealed laws for they are appropriate to every age and society. By combining the inner knowledge of and awakening to the divine purpose with the outer laws, which are general yet include specific instructions for transaction, conduct and worship, the 'package' was complete.

Initially this complete version of Islam was adopted by the Arab tribes of western Arabia and within a few decades had swept into the eastern Byzantine and Sassanian Empires. Wherever Islam was embraced its impact was to refine, purify and modify the existing culture, creating a certain common harmonious pattern, yet without imposing cultural uniformity. Outer differences were sustained by a unique foundation of faith and submission to a mighty, compassionate and everlasting Creator.

THE WORLD IN THE SEVENTH CENTURY

The historical landscape in which the last message of Islam arose was made up of four major empires. Around the middle of the seventh century CE the civilized or 'ruled' world consisted of the Byzantine Empire with its centre in Constantinople, the Sassanian with its centre in Ctesiphon (present-day Baghdad), the Hindu Empire in north India, and the Chinese Empire. Movement, change and dynamism seemed to be centred around the eastern shores of the Mediterranean where decades of warfare, commerce and other interaction took place between the worlds of Roman Christianity, the Sassanians and other Christian and Jewish communities in East Africa and other parts of the Arabian peninsula.

The Roman Empire, which had officially embraced Christianity from the early fourth century, had the New Testament written in Greek, thereby remoulding Hellenistic art, philosophy, science and law into a Christian format. Byzantine rule from Constantinople emerged as a Hellenistic – Christian hybrid quite different from the original Christianity emanating from the Fertile Crescent. Constantinople had replaced Rome as the centre of the Roman Empire because it was closer geographically to the central axis of communication and economic exchange. Greek was the Empire's language of high culture, while Latin was used for law; and Gregory the Great, the Pope of Rome, was subject to imperial rule from Constantinople.

Everyday life differed greatly from place to place between cities and the rural parts of the Empire. A few communities (such as the Nestorians) were still living and following an early Christian or gnostically oriented way of life, whereas the majority had become hedonistic and worldly. Several communities in North Africa and elsewhere within the Empire held on to a unitarian system of belief under Roman rule. The peak of Roman Christian orthodoxy, power and culture was reached during the reign of Justinian (527–565).

During the first few decades of the seventh century Sassanian rule had expanded considerably into Egypt, and Syria and Anatolia were taken by Khusraw Parviz. The Sassanian Empire was based on rule by an absolute monarch who had risen above the ordinary people's ambition and greed so that he could establish peace and justice for the subjected people. Zoroaster was revered as the Supreme Prophet, and court rule was sustained by a landowning nobility and a priestly hierarchy. This was in contrast to the Roman Empire, where the tradesmen – merchant class provided the support.

The struggle between the Romans and the Sassanians had been going on since Alexander the Great's conquest in the fourth century, and the early decades of the seventh century marked the obvious decline and weakening of both these old empires as a result of their continuous war and confrontation. In 629 the True Cross was restored to Jerusalem, symbolizing the triumph of Christianity over the Zoroastrian Empire, the Jews and deviants from the established creed.

The Zoroastrian Sassanian Empire had harboured considerable numbers of Christians. Its written language was Pahlavi (an Indo-Iranian language) though Aramaic was also widely used. The relationships between these varied peoples and their contacts with the Indians and Chinese developed mainly along the trade routes criss-crossing the land from east to west, and occasionally north to south, by a mercantile class bringing goods and cultural influences from the Nile to the Oxus. It was the same commercial class of people plying these routes that later helped spread the new spiritual awakening of Islam.

The religious and cultural beliefs prevalent in India and China at that time were variations on Hindu and Buddhist teachings respectively. Their spiritual beliefs emphasized mastering the self and understanding existence through adherence to a code of non-violence, deep meditation and enlightenment. The Indic cultures focused particularly upon personal salvation with secondary importance given to rule and outer law. In contrast to this, the Hellenistic thinkers and the Christians who adopted Hellenism, explored the external nature of outer phenomena and the moral nature of the individual.

ARABS AND ARABIA

The Arabian Peninsula was inhabited by Arabic-speaking Bedouin tribes living a nomadic life. They criss-crossed various settlements in valleys and oases, concentrating on areas near the western coast of the Red Sea and along the trade routes between Yemen and Damascus. The word 'Arab' originally meant nomadic Bedouin and only later came to include all those who spoke the language or absorbed Arab culture.

Life in Arabia was tribal, punctuated by frequent inter-clan and inter-tribal warfare as well as raids on trade caravans and settlements. The nomadic code of conduct was based on tribal loyalty, pride in ancestry and a great deal of personal independence. Tribal leadership was not necessarily directly inherited, but to a great extent earned by general consensus and acknowledgement of the leader's qualities. Each tribe was sovereign unto itself. Social stability was based on loyalty to the clan rather than on any political form. Any attack therefore on any member of the group was regarded as an attack on the whole group, resulting in tribal animosities that were sometimes carried into urban life. The Arab sense of tribal or clannish belonging, pride in genealogy, love of independence, and defiance of outside authority have remained their predominant characteristics to this day.

For the sake of simplicity, the distinction between northern and southern tribes is a useful one. The northern tribes of 'Adnan included the major tribes that inhabited the Gezira, the western and central parts of Arabia as well as most of those in southern Iraq. Parts of the southern or Yemeni tribes of Qahtan had spread into Syria and Iraq under the names of *Kalb* and *Kindah*. Much of the later in-fighting between the Arab Muslims in Andalusia can be understood if one bears in mind the nature of tribal allegiance. Numerous rulers in Andalusia and elsewhere often used ancestry and blood ties to justify rulership.

Many Arabian tribes were involved in commerce between the Mediterranean and the southern seas, carrying goods and safeguarding them between the commercial centres of Damascus and the southern port of Mocha (Aden). Others made their living by raiding caravans or settlements, or by leading a pastoral life, herding camels, sheep and goats. The herdsmen were constantly on the move between the infrequent wells, springs and oases. This kind of existence was only possible because of the domesticated camel which combined ease of mobility with the ability to endure harsh conditions. In addition to being a great beast of burden, the camel could be milked and its hair and dung used.

Camel nomadism was only possible because of a highly specialized form of social organization in which the honour of the individual was held uppermost. Generosity was considered the highest virtue. The social prestige of a Bedouin was directly proportionate to his dependence on animals: the greater their number and size, the greater his potential for mobility and therefore his esteem. Able to travel long distances through the desert, the camel freed the Bedouins from agrarian controls and gave them mastery over desert and oasis. Even those who eventually settled in agricultural oases or commercial towns tended to perpetuate the same principles of social organization, maintaining their camels nearby, still cherishing their heritage as free wanderers, or at the very least, as pastoralists.

The language of these Arabs who dominated the Arabian Peninsula was, of course, Arabic, the Semitic cousin of Aramaic. The earliest Arab inscriptions which date back to the fourth century CE were mostly written in the Aramaic script, Arabic script evolving later. Poetry was the most striking feature of Arab creative expression, for, being truly portable, the human voice declaiming poems was the ultimate nomadic form of artistic activity. Their powers of memory were therefore well exercised and developed, an important point to note given the nature of the later revelation of the Qur'an.

The system of belief in most of the Arabian peoples was in one form or another pagan, with varying degrees of influence from the Christian and Jewish communities that lived both within Arabia and in the lands to the north and south.

In the mountainous southern Arabian peninsula the dominant culture and religion of the Yemen was Christian, with smaller numbers of Jews and pagans present. The Abyssinian culture which derived from Yemen had over time developed its own flavour and it is because of these historical ties between Yemen and Ethiopia that Abyssinian Christianity prevailed in the horn of Africa.

The small town of Mecca was the most important trading centre in the west of the peninsula because it sat at the junction of the two major routes: one north-south connecting Syria and the Mediterranean to Yemen and the lands beyond the Indian Ocean, the other east-west from Iraq and Iran to Africa and the Mediterranean. It had been a prominent and prestigious town since ancient times.

Arab paganism focused on worship at the cubic structure of the Ka'bah, known as the House of God, and originally built by the Prophet Abraham. This institutionalized religion brought about a certain measure of solidarity among the Arabs and a focal point for identification with their numerous deities, most of which were associated with natural objects, stones and stars. Sacred tokens of all clans were gathered in the Ka'bah, and the ritual of circling around it and touching the Black Stone lodged into one corner was a time-revered practice. Superstition, however, abounded, as did an enormous variety of beliefs and methods of worship. Some people even went around the Ka'bah naked, while at times the sacred water of the well of Zam-Zam was polluted as much by neglect as by lawlessness, incivility and the low level of hygiene. Since this major ritual was not exclusive to any one faith, many Christians, Jews and Sabaeans also sent offerings and performed the rituals. Though it was not unusual for each tribe to adopt a favourite deity, Allah was regarded by all Arabians as the Highest or Creator God.

MUHAMMAD IN MECCA

It was into this background that the final prophetic message of Islam was revealed. Within less than half a century it sparked off the most rapidly growing religious revitalization and civilization, embracing numerous peoples from remote areas with diverse cultural backgrounds. The wave of Islam swept eastwards into Iran and the Fertile Crescent as well as westwards into the land of the Byzantines and North Africa.

Muhammad was born in AD 570 into the clan of Hashim (Banu Hashim) of the tribe of Quraysh, who at that time were the most powerful and prestigious tribe in Mecca. Some generations before Muhammad's birth, the Quraysh had taken over the guardianship of the Shrine of the Ka'bah and the springs at Mecca, and had since ruled through clan council. It was the scion of his clan, his grandfather 'Abd ul-Muttalib, who became Muhammad's guardian when he was orphaned.

By the time Muhammad turned twenty, he had already participated in several long trade voyages as well as a few tribal expeditions and wars. His impeccable conduct had earned him an outstanding reputation for uprightness, honesty and nobility. These qualities attracted Khadijah, a wealthy lady from a prominent Meccan family, who was fifteen years his senior. Muhammad married her at the age of twenty-five, and this union was most significant in the support, solace and companionship they shared, particularly in the early days of his prophethood. Although Muhammad was not a vocal rebel against his community's social and institutional life, throughout his youth he clearly dissociated himself from the pagan rites and customs of the Quraysh. He had no spiritual or other formal education and no background in the Judaic and Christian traditions. He had, however, spent much time meditating for long periods in a mountain cave outside Mecca, called Hira.

His final spiritual awakening and call to prophethood occurred when he was about forty. The event of the full revelation was as dramatic and sudden as it was transformative. The human frame is too frail to absorb the shock of the infinite unveiled Light of Reality, so for the next twenty-three years of his life the revealed message of the Qur'an descended upon the Prophet through the angelic medium of Gabriel. There is no doubt that neither the occasion nor the content of the revealed message was under Muhammad's conscious control. The sequence of the revelation followed an organic pattern dictated by the occasion, but Muhammad already knew the form of the whole Qur'an, which he clarified after it was fully revealed before his death.

The particular night that the Qur'an descended upon the Prophet's heart is described as the 'Night of Power' (laylat al-qadr; 97:1–5), symbolizing the full descent of the Book of Knowledge in contrast to the years it took for it to be outwardly manifested.

Another night of note which is regarded as a significant experience in the Prophet's life was the 'Night of Ascent' (laylat al-mi'raj; 17:1), in which the Prophet actually experienced a heavenward journey that included a pilgrimage to Jerusalem. Natural physical limitations were overcome and the soul's journey to its Lord took place. This event is symbolically reflected in the transportation of the believer's soul during his or her daily prayers.

Muhammad's mission and the message of the Qur'an presented a great challenge to the Meccans. This challenge remains as forceful to this day. Those who accepted his message during the first years were very few. In addition to his loyal wife Khadijah, his cousin, Ali Ibn Abi Talib, and Zayd Ibn Harithah (both youths living in his own household) stood behind him. Abu Bakr, a well-known Meccan merchant, and a handful of others soon followed, together with a number of youths, slaves and other tribeless people.

The rest of Muhammad's tribe soon became hostile to him and his mission for it challenged their existing idolatry and pagan social practices. His teachings threatened to undermine the entire way of life of the Arab peoples. His call to submit, adore, worship and fear the One and Only God and to abandon all other false worldly bases of security and power were too much to bear for these clannish pagans. Arab nomadic society was, after all, founded upon ancestral tradition and depended on the exercise of strength and cunning for its survival.

The Qur'anic revelation during this period was mostly related to the knowledge of God, self-purification and abandonment, and submission to the infinite and all-encompassing Reality. The Meccan revelations emphasized human salvation, awakening to mankind's divine origin, fear of God and the Last Judgement.

The increasing hostilities waged against the Muslims and the Prophet in Mecca resulted in the migration of some seventy of his followers to the friendly protection of the neighbouring Christian King of Abyssinia. Soon afterwards, and as a result of friendly invitations for him to migrate to the nearby town of Yathrib, Muhammad departed secretly from Mecca under cover of night accompanied by his closest companion Abu Bakr. His cousin, (and by now son-in-law) 'Ali, was left behind that night to sleep in the Prophet's bed so as to foil the plot of a band of Quraysh who had been intending to murder him while he slept. Within days the Prophet and his followers were installed in their new base and thus began the new phase of his life and mission, establishing a spiritually guided community.

LIVING ISLAM: THE MEDINA MODEL

On 24th September CE 622 the Prophet entered Yathrib, a city predominantly inhabited by two Arab tribes and a community of Jews. This migration (*Hijrah*) later became the starting point for the Muslim lunar calendar.

Yathrib became the home of the first living community of Muslims. Islam is a *Din*, a life-transaction. The first place this action began to unfold was subsequently called Medina, for this name is derived from the word meaning to civilize or refine, implying that civilization takes root where the *Din* is practised.

In Medina the Prophet established and led the new community. He was naturally selected as the divinely inspired 'philosopher-king' who had transcended the limitations of Self and Ego and had thereby become the perfect interspace between the material world and the world beyond time and space.

The early years were marked by numerous defensive battles to ward off the attacks of the Quraysh and other tribes. Although Muhammad taught his community to defend themselves and fight in the way of God, he also constantly reminded them of the necessity for inner purification and self-abandonment in order to reflect the attributes of Divine Mercy.

Throughout his time in Medina Muhammad led the life of an ordinary man, acting as father, husband and member of the community, yet he was distinguished above all mankind by receiving the inspirational Message directly from the Divine Source. He lived in the moment without reference to the disturbances and injuries of the past, and without fear of the future, except for what pleased God and met with His approval and will.

By the eighth year in Medina the community had begun to outgrow its physical boundaries and started to expand as new converts joined them during their pilgrimages to Mecca. Soon afterwards the Meccans capitulated and gave in to the swelling wave of Islam. The idols in the Ka'bah were destroyed and the mercy of Islam encompassed all those who entered it in peace. During the last two years of the Prophet's life thousands of tribal Arabs, Jews and others, embraced Islam, either out of conviction or convenience. Among those who did so at the last hour were some of Muhammad's fiercest enemies who in later decades reverted to some of their pagan tribal habits.

It is estimated that between the years 7 and 10 after *Hijrah* (AH) the number of Muslims grew from tens of thousands to over two hundred thousand. Many of the new adherents had very little time or opportunity (and sometimes even lacked the inclination) to learn about this total system of life-transaction. By the tenth year AH large numbers of warring tribes, from the north and south, from Yemen and Syria, Persians, rich, poor, black, white, meek and mighty, were all sheltered and absorbed by Islam.

Towards the end of the tenth year AH the Prophet performed the first complete Islamic pilgrimage, the rituals and formalities of which are followed to this day. On his return from

Mecca to Medina he proclaimed that 'Ali was his heir and successor at Ghadir Khum. This proclamation, however, was interpreted by different factions in different ways, such as to mean 'Ali was the spiritual inheritor rather than the political heir. This event was a major turning point in the history of the Muslims, for from it grew the division between Shi'is and Sunnis (see Chapters Four and Five).

After the Prophet's return to Medina from Hajj he fell ill, and after a few days of fever his soul departed on the 13th of *Rabi' al-Awwal* (the third month of the Muslim calendar year).

As we have already seen, the nature of the Qur'anic message in Mecca was to do with faith, belief, trust in and submission to Allah, selflessly, generously living this life in preparation for the next. In the Medina phase, however, the revealed message and prophetic actions dealt mostly with matters of community, family and social life, trade, war, law and all the other regulatory foundations required for a civilized society. It was in Medina that most of the acts of worship and the ordinances governing social order were revealed. The revelations and prophetic teachings during this period later gave rise to the development of Islamic theology and jurisprudence, and all the other scholarship of a formalized religion.

It was in Medina that the Qur'an showed clearly that Islam is not simply a matter of individual enlightenment and obedience to God; but includes a foundation for a wholesome community in which all Muslims are bound to each other through honourable and accountable conduct. Indeed, it is only under these circumstances that individual awakening can be enhanced and supported.

The Qur'an describes the life of the community in Medina as the most perfect that has been brought into existence: 'And the believers, men and women, are friends of one another; they enjoin the good and forbid evil . . .' (9:71). The ultimate good is worship and knowledge of Allah, and the worst evil is selfishness, ignorance and the pretension of having no need of Allah.

The Medina model is a way of life in harmony with all creation and its Creator. Its fabric is woven of a life-transaction that unifies the constant personal struggle towards inner purification with awareness of outer change and the ever-present tendencies of the ego-self. Its social fibres are composed of deep courtesy and responsibility towards others. The model of Medina symbolizes the practice ground for self-awakening, the social expression and living achievement of true Islam.

The life of Medina followed the spiritual enlightenment of Mecca. The communal aspects of our lives follow those of personal awakening. When the inner reality has been discovered then the outer law and courtesy will be established as a natural consequence. Mecca relates to perfecting inner ecology, while Medina relates to interacting with the outer environment. Mecca was the unveiling of the microcosm, Medina was the living macrocosm.

THE WAY OF MUHAMMAD: THE PERFECT MODEL

This day have I perfected for you your religion and completed my favour to you and chosen for you Islam as a religion.

Qur'an 5:3

The natural development of the self-awakened is to move from the discovery of the Divine Light within oneself – serving others with humility, selflessness and love – to the Creational Source that is behind all creational manifestation. After the retreat into the cave of awakening comes the return to society. After having been illuminated and having tamed the lower animalistic tendencies, one can only re-connect with the natural creation, the highest manifestation of which is humankind.

The life of the Prophet and his experiences encompass a rich source of teaching for those who want to follow in the prophetic footsteps, for he underwent practically every possible human experience as he fulfilled the roles of teacher, immigrant, merchant, head of the household, political and social leader, military commander, judge, ruler and, throughout, the Seal of the Prophets. His nobility, humanity, magnanimity, courage, forgiveness, steadfastness, understanding and total devotion to Allah, the Most Glorious, were expressed in such diverse situations common to the collective experience of mankind. His behaviour and conduct, the *Sunnah*, became the ideal standard to be followed and from it the adjective

17

Sunni is derived. In this sense every Muslim aspires to be a *Sunni*, that is, he or she aims to follow the Prophet's way.

His love for children and his loving conduct towards his daughter Fatima and his wives, as well as his care for orphans and the needy were all glowing examples for his contemporaries and also for latter-day Muslims. He was always spontaneous, accessible, selflessly devoted to serving God's creation cheerfully and with no worldly expectation. His inner joy and tranquillity radiated while he exerted outer effort and struggle to uplift humanity towards fulfilling its highest potential. His sincerity to the cause of unveiling the truth, his total reliability and other virtuous characteristics revealed themselves even in the most adverse of circumstances.

Muhammad's way was the perfection of the prophetic way that began with the rise of consciousness in the Adamic model. The revealed Qur'an talks about all the Prophets and Messengers as having brought to their communities the one and only message of abandonment into God, living a godly way in this physical existence before returning to another phase of being.

The Qur'an acknowledges all the Prophets. From other traditions we are subsequently told that there were thousands of them (the figure of 124,000 is given), but of them only a few were referred to in the Qur'an. In fact, there are far more references to the Prophets Moses and Jesus than to Muhammad. Though it makes no distinction between them, the Qur'an does highlight those that brought about crucial social change as those possessed of resolution (*ulu' al'azm*; 46:35), and these include Abraham, Noah, Moses, Jesus and Muhammad.

Muhammad is the culminating pinnacle of all the Prophets and Messengers. He embodies the completion of the collective prophetic consciousness that has come to mankind during the years of the final evolution and awakening of the higher consciousness within the human being. His message confirms all that went before and points out where distortion, misunderstanding and aberration have occurred. Thus his message supersedes all those previous to it in a way that leaves no space for any doubt or misunderstanding, except for those who actively seek it and wish to create confusion for themselves and others.

THE LIVING QUR'AN

Although the Qur'an is a treasury of information, its real glory and miracle lie in its power to transform those who approach it with faith and the conviction that it is the revealed divine blueprint. It unveils itself and clarifies what appears to be obscure in some parts by other sections within it. The organic interrelationship of all its topics reflects reality in such a way that it defies a purely structuralist scholastic approach. As the manifestation of the highest godly attributes in human form, the Prophet was described as the 'Living Qur'an'. He considered all Prophets and Messengers his brothers. Indeed, he considered all mankind a single brotherhood, all men and women being equal in the eyes of the Creator, but those are most honoured by the Creator who are most pious and sincere in their submission and abandonment.

The Qur'an reveals that all the Prophets are in Islam, each one of them moving along this path of awakening (22:78). The greatest patriarch and early Prophet of the Judaic-Christian-Islamic continuum, the Prophet Abraham, declared: 'I submit myself to the Lord of the worlds' (2:131), referring to his discovery of the way to arrival through submission. Most of the Prophets of the Bani (tribe of) Israel who are mentioned in the Qur'an declare the same, as did Noah: 'I am commanded to be of those who submit' (10:72).

The Qur'an describes that the only way as far as Allah is concerned is Islam; any other path will not be accepted from man. This is to say that whoever does not enter the ultimate sanctuary through its door will be obstructed, because the ultimate sanctuary is based on the unity of the Creator, and as long as the seeker still sees himself, his method, his 'way' as important, he will not arrive at that final realization.

During his stay in Mecca, the Prophet only spoke about God and what He desires of His creation, what pleases Him and the ways that deflect and distract one from Him. During the thirteen years of the Meccan period, the prophetic message focused on self-enlightenment based on selfless action and reflection. The Qur'an confirms that when guidance comes from Allah or when God wishes to guide someone, his or her heart will be opened or their burdens will be lifted through this submission (6:125). So it is by faith and trust that there arises in the believer the natural state of active awareness and spontaneous purification which is the result of the path of submission, thereby unifying personal acts of worship and morality with that of communal responsibility.

Muhammad's way was that of love for and submission to the one and only Creator, and consideration for all creation. It was the way of being a guest in this short life in order to move into the higher realm of afterlife. The Muhammadi model of existence is based on the truth that human life is born out of a fusion between the spirit, which is from beyond time and space (for it is from the Divine Command), and physical matter resulting in the individual soul. This event comes about in order to complete the journey of the soul from its Creator via creation back to Creator. It is part of the process of the final awakening to the one and only Reality in existence.

True freedom comes through recognizing the transience of all physical experience. Since human beings cannot derive security from anything transient, they must seek the non-transient which lies only within the heart.

> Heavens and earth do not contain Me but the heart of the believer contains Me.
>
> (Sacred Tradition)

The Muhammadi model shows us that this awakening occurs when the heart is purified and emptied of all idols like the Ka'bah, for it is the ultimate sanctuary. If there are false gods in it then there is no room for Allah. Only through purity of heart is that spontaneous awareness and intuition heightened and with that the human being becomes the interfacing locus between the seen and the unseen.

2 · FAITH AND PATH

> Whatever is in the heavens and earth declares the glory of Allah, and He is the Mighty, the Wise.
>
> Qur'an 57:1

The Qur'an reveals that all creation adores and worships the Creator, which is the very purpose of creation. All outer physical realities have been created from a unique essence which encompasses all these realities in their changing manifestation. The Qur'an further reveals that in every instance and in every experience Allah manifests in a different fashion (55:29). We are also told that Allah created humankind from one self and from it created its pair (7:189). This self has been given a choice of either rising to its divine origin or allowing itself to become corrupted in this world and then suffering in the hereafter.

The creation from one self implies that all human beings share a unique primal model. The spirit is from beyond time and space and therefore beyond reason and understanding. When this spirit combines with sentient matter in the womb it produces the individualized self. Within each self is reflected the spectrum of all mineral, vegetable, animal and higher faculties of cognition. The self is programmed to seek harmony, balance, good health, a tranquil mind and friendly companionship, thus seeking what is pleasing to it and desiring protection from what is not. It is these fundamental characteristics of the one self that inherently motivate us.

21

Apparent differences among mankind are in the main due to our genetic inheritances and other superficially distinguishing characteristics.

Success, and therefore fulfilment, of all life's experience is to be guided by reason and inspired by faith and subtler knowledge. Despite experiencing the undesirable, if we have faith and if we have exercised reason fully then faith will enable us to see the benefit of whatever situation we are in, even that of ill-health or a reversal in fortune.

The purpose of creation is at all times to be exposed to the Essence, which is indescribable yet ever-present, beyond reason and intellect. This is the zone of gnosis or awakening to the unseen through the heart.

The path of Islam is based on the middle way: the Muslim outwardly applies reason, justice, compassion and all other virtues while inwardly he or she is in abandonment and submission, trusting that the outcome to any situation will be the appropriate one. Therefore, whoever is in true and constant submission, in utmost awareness both outwardly and inwardly, is on the path of pursuing the ultimate knowledge and fulfilling their purpose.

The Creator God is hidden behind all our projects, actions and worldly involvements. He is not subject to time or space nor is He subject to any change such as we experience. Since the Infinite Essence echoes within us, we can put up with the world of experience only when we ourselves have awakened to an inner state that is beyond time and space.

ELEMENTS OF THE *DIN*

> Surely the [true] religion with Allah is Islam. And those who were given the Book differed only after knowledge had come to them, out of envy among themselves.
>
> Qur'an 3:19

No word in English is adequate to convey the all-encompassing nature of the word *Din*, which is most commonly translated as 'religion'. The root of the word *Din* relates to obedience and following and to owing or being indebted. The *Din* of Islam envelops a total pattern of transaction with oneself, creation and the Creator. To follow, submit and comply with the truth is the only appropriate way to act in this creation.

According to the Qur'an, all Prophets and Messengers were in Allah's *Din*; they were all therefore in Islam (22:78). However, there appear to be different religions if one looks at the historical progress of mankind. We cannot say that all these religions are one for they have come at different times, with different cultural understanding as well as with different outer rituals and laws (22:67). The correct, appropriate life-transaction at the time of Moses was Judaic, at the time of Jesus it was Christian and at the time of Muhammad was what has come to be know as Islam. Judaism and Christianity were the Islam of their time. The last version of Islam, however, supersedes and encompasses all previous models in all aspects.

As the number and diversity of Muslims rapidly grew during the first and second centuries after *Hijrah*, the need for a consistent and encapsulated teaching of the *Din* became necessary. Islamic theology and jurisprudence developed in response to this need. The simple Islamic religious teaching soon began to develop procedures and formats for referencing and authenticating the teachings, and this included the basic distinction between the foundation of the *Din* and its practices and rituals.

FOUNDATIONS OF THE *DIN*

The first foundation of belief – the creed or *shahadah* (literally testimony) – is that there is no god but the One God and that Muhammad is His Messenger. There is only one unique, ultimate high Reality, and that One God reflects in attributes, the most beautiful of which are the ninety-nine names mentioned in the Qur'an (such as the Beneficent, *ar-Rahman*; the All-Seeing, *al-Basir*; the Expander, *al-Basit*). God's total attributes, however, cannot be counted. The Qur'an says:

> And if all the trees in the earth were pens and the sea with seven more seas added to it [were ink], the words of Allah would not be exhausted; surely Allah is Mighty, Wise.
>
> Qur'an 31:27

With belief in Allah comes belief in His absolute Power and therefore the realms of the unseen which contain those subtle agents, His Angels.

The second fundamental element of faith is divine justice. Allah is absolutely just. Justice in this world, however, is relative because of man's interference which brings about injustice. If one is not given the appropriate reward or punishment in this world, the process will continue after death, until justice has prevailed to encompass the worlds of both the seen and unseen.

The third foundation of belief is that of prophethood. From the Higher Reality numerous Prophets and Messengers have come in order to raise human consciousness to that higher awareness and knowledge. Coming at different times and to different people, these beings have always imparted the same message but with slightly varying outer practices appropriate to their times. Muhammad embodies all previous teachings and as far as outer practice is concerned he supersedes them all. After Muhammad there will be no change because there can be no improvement on what was revealed to him for it is applicable and usable at all times by all people in all circumstances. With the completion of the collective prophetic consciousness in Muhammad, attaining inner transformation has become easier and accessible to everyone, provided the teachings and practices of the Qur'an and the way of the Prophet are adhered to.

The fourth element relates to spiritual leadership and the necessity of combining the spiritual with the secular. The Prophet Muhammad was the supreme example of this for he was the governor as well as the foremost spiritual guide of his time. Every society needs to follow a leader, and the most worthy to lead is he who combines godly qualities (gnosis) with acknowledged abilities and virtues. Recognition of this need forms the basis for imamate, which is that society should be led by the foremost among men (imam literally means he who stands in front, as in leading the prayers). It is in this matter that Sunnis and Shi'is differ, which is explained on pages 58–62.

The last element of faith is the 'return': the belief that the soul lives on in another phase of existence after the death

of the body. In the hereafter the soul will live by whatever
it has attained and achieved by means of its intentions and
actions in this world. Since neither time nor space apply in
the afterlife, the state of the soul with which one enters that
zone will resonate forever. The return to Source is therefore
conditioned by existence in the physical world.

CREATION

His command, when He intends anything, is only to say to it,
'Be', and it is.

Qur'an 36:82

All creation has come about from the command 'Be'. The
Qur'an describes how the world of solidity has come about
from a fluid and gaseous substance, before which there was
nothing but the void from which the command came. The
return to that original point of emanation is also described
(19:40, 41:21).

As for the purpose of creation, Allah says in a sacred
tradition, 'I was a hidden treasure and I loved to be known,
therefore I created so that I might be known.' The primary
purpose of creation is to know the Creator.

Wherever you turn, there is the face of Allah.

Qur'an 2:115

At every instant, in every period and every day, He manifests
in a different way. Creation is the act of Allah emanating
from His infinite attributes, all of which are founded on His
Unique Essence.

Creation follows a certain prescribed path or decree to meet
its final destiny. Every physical entity is subject to natural
laws and limitations. Its destiny is determined according to its
interaction with the multitudes of laws at play. As far as human
choice is concerned, we can choose to expose ourselves to
certain situations and their concomitant governing laws rather
than others. If, for example, one acts with fear, pessimism and

neglect, then the outcome of the action will in all probability be failure. We need to consider, therefore, all the laws that affect a particular situation and apply these 'decrees' until the final destiny is achieved.

Allah's revelation in the Qur'an and the prophetic teachings highlight the importance of developing the faculty of cognition and reasoning. The prophetic advice is to take reasoning to its limit and then depend on Allah with positive faith, trust and the highest expectation of the right (i.e. best) outcome.

The Qur'an also gives us examples, assurances and explanations of other creations such as angels and jinn. Made of light, angels have no choice but to follow their prescribed patterning, whereas jinn, who are made of fire and air, reflect their elemental volatility in virtuous or evil behaviour.

Allah says in the Qur'an that every person is responsible and accountable for his or her own actions and for the extent to which he or she has realized the purpose of existence. He says that 'If you bring to life one person it is as though you have brought to life the entire creation, and if you kill one person you have killed the entire creation.' This underlines the unitive, creational reality behind the multiplicity of observed or experienced creation. The highest goal is to bring forth life – enlightened, awakened, 'real' life as distinct from purely biological sentience. It is as though this life is a nursery in which we are all being taught the ultimate knowledge of the One, All-Permeating Reality which is the source of life as experienced in this world.

The Qur'an repeatedly reminds us of a post-death future existence the experience of which will be shaped by our actions in this world, the zone of action and interaction. Our actions and the intentions behind them will be relived in the next life which is subject neither to time nor space. We may justify or give reasons for our inappropriate or selfish actions and intentions, but excuses will be of no use or benefit when we are finally confronted with the Ultimate Reality.

Thus we participate in scripting our future life after death by our actions in this world. If we live a life of true faith and submission to Allah, acting with full responsibility, selflessly, honourably and virtuously, then we are moving along the intended path for success that will be tasted both now and later.

MICROCOSM: HUMANKIND

He created you from a single being, then made its mate of the same kind.

Qur'an 39:6

The most important creation is our own self. The self is programmed to want to discover its nature. Who are we? Why do we experience fluctuating moods? What makes us desire security, wealth, long life and inner equilibrium?

The prophetic model of the origin and development of the self teaches us that spirit acts upon matter, and results in a soul which lives within the physical body, which in turn integrates biological, physiological, mental and intellectual components. We experience the gross, physical body as well as the subtler mental and higher cognitive faculties. The human self includes all these constituents and the experiences that come through them. Knowledge of the self, therefore, is based on understanding these various facets.

The self is bracketed at one end with divine light-spirit, and at the other by the physical, earthy body which contains elements of all that is in nature – mineral, vegetal or animal. The whole range of possible behaviour has been given to the self, from the most degenerate to the most virtuous and divine. It is only through purification of the heart, however, that the self takes on the colour of the divine.

Allah tells us in the Qur'an that He has not given any man two hearts in his breast (33:4), which means that if we want a pure heart we cannot clutter it with desires, fears and other impurities. At the same time if we wish to accumulate worldly effects, then that is where the heart will take us. If we seek higher knowledge and Divine Light, then that too is where the heart will take us. We move in either one direction or another, for two arrows cannot be sprung from the bow simultaneously.

We can describe the body, mind and intellect, but when it comes to higher awareness, we are unable to reason or analyse this central zone of the heart. The Qur'an refers to the heart on numerous occasions:

> O you who believe! Answer [the call of] Allah and His Apostle when He calls you to that which brings you life; and know that Allah intervenes between man and his heart, and that to Him you shall be gathered.
>
> Qur'an 8:24

The Qur'an also tells us that it is only through remembrance of Allah that hearts achieve contentment (13:28). Allah describes those who succeed in coming to spiritual life and who fear the Beneficent God as those of gentle and repentant hearts. The hearts is the purest filter and organ of understanding:

> Have they not travelled in the land so that they should have hearts with which to understand or ears with which to hear? For surely it is not the eyes that are blind, but blind are the hearts which are in their breasts. (22:46)

Higher inner understanding and cognition occur when the heart is healthy and able to receive the relevant inspiration.

The self is journeying in this world, both physically and metaphorically. This journey can be along a clear road based on rationality and an inspired pure heart which will lead to self-knowledge, or along a confused road bent with anger, frustration and disappointment.

Allah, the All-Merciful, reminds us in the Qur'an that while His mercy pervades every situation and experience it is the individual who fashions his or her world (7:156). Indeed, the Garden of the Fire of the hereafter is being rehearsed and produced by our own conduct in this world. We are each our own film-maker; we are the actor, director, cameraman, producer and audience, but this can only be understood if we stop identifying ourselves with the myriad roles we act out in this life. On the final day, nothing will veil us from seeing ourselves as we really are.

> The day on which wealth will not avail, nor offspring, except him who comes to Allah with a sound [pure] heart
>
> Qur'an 26:88–89

Thus it is by means of the quality of heart that human worth is ultimately judged.

Self-awakening is the realization and understanding of all the different aspects that the self experiences. Self-knowledge is related to the knowledge of the cause of selfhood and its essence, not the various attributes or experiences that come about from it. Self-knowledge will at all times enable us to see the unifying cause – the Unific Source – behind diverse and opposite manifestations.

The Prophet said, 'Whoever knows his self knows his Lord.' The choice is ours, for it is only we who carve our destiny according to the natural laws and subtler decrees that Allah has provided in His creational design. Knowledge of the self is the highest of all knowledges for it leads to knowledge of the Lord. That knowledge will also enable us to understand the rest of creation, because the microcosm is but a paradigm of the macrocosm.

MACROCOSM: THE NATURAL WORLD

Allah is the light of the heavens and the earth. A likeness of His light is as a pillar on which is a lamp – the lamp is in a glass, the glass is as it were a brightly shining star – lit from a blessed olive tree, neither eastern nor western, the oil whereof gives light, though fire touch it not – light upon light. Allah guides to His light whom He pleases. And Allah sets forth parables for men, and Allah is Knower of all things.

Qur'an 24:35

The world at large is the mirror in which we reflect ourselves. It is the macrocosm in which the individual self, the microcosm, discovers itself. In the same way that the outer world has a creational beginning and end, so too does the self. To understand the outer world we need to understand the self, and to understand the self we need to interact with the outer world. To understand one's own individuality one must look at the individuality of others, for the original creational pattern is one and the same, although outer action or manifestation appear diverse.

All worldly experience is based on opposites: it is either day or night, sweet or sour, hot or cold, man or woman, exhaling or inhaling, desirable or undesirable. Whatever action we undertake is either to summon something we desire (the force of attraction) or to ward off something we do not desire (the force of repulsion). The entire creation is based on emanation and return, the two existential opposites based on an unchanging foundation of unity, the One Unique Essence, Allah.

The world is subject to natural physical laws, and the creations within it experience and interact both with the individual entity of their own self and with the larger entity of the world. In each situation we constantly try to bring about a certain equilibrium between ourselves and the impinging world, the measure of which is known within each self.

Islam teaches us the laws both of the inner self and of the outer world. Both the Qur'an and the Prophet's Sunnah (way) indicate that there is an optimum way of dealing with the self as well as its larger reflection. This optimum way is the foundation, the teachings of which later came to be collected and called the Shari'ah (literally 'way' or 'road'), or Law.

Made up as it is of divine revelation and prophetic practice, the Shari'ah focuses on personal as well as environmental hygiene, both literally and metaphorically. We are told to take from this world only what is necessary for our outer journey through it. We are warned against greed and the accumulation of wealth or possessions. The Qur'an constantly encourages generosity and trust, while the prophetic teaching is very much based on taking little in order to give more. The path of Islam is made up of piety, asceticism, courtesy and struggle in the way of Allah and the Prophet.

In order for society to exist and for civilization to flourish, it is necessary to have outer prescriptions delineating certain limits. The outer laws govern human interaction and the social order, as well as our interaction with other creatures and the environment, thus preserving the ecological balance. To live healthily we need to eat well and therefore to take from the earth what we need. But we are warned against excesses in food, clothing or shelter. For example, we are not permitted to hunt or kill animals, nor are we permitted to wear their skins, unless they were expressly killed for the purpose of eating. In any case, only a few animals and birds are permitted for this purpose. Using animals for entertainment or in any manner that is not natural to them is also forbidden. Interaction with nature is based on taking from it the minimum necessary for life to continue. Respect for nature is respect for the Creator.

The macrocosm of the world is the training ground in which the grooming of the self takes place, the nursery in which humanity can strive to fulfil its purpose. The world is the Medina of mankind, for it is here that we discharge the debt upon ourselves to discover the origin of our higher self. By understanding the self within, we will come to understand the universe, for the inner universe is a true compact replica of the vast outer universe. If we start with the microcosm we shall end up with the macrocosm and vice versa, for the two are only manifestations of the One.

UNICOSM: THE ALL-PERVADING REALITY

For the purposes of describing the greater cosmic reality which permeates and encompasses both the microcosm and the macrocosm, we have taken the liberty of coining a new term: the unicosm. The relationship between the unicosm, the individual being and the world at large is such that they are interlinked both discernibly and in the unseen. Each individual experiences the outer material world as well as the inner world which is more subtle and therefore less controllable or definable. Every part of the created world possesses an inner and an outer aspect.

The unicosm refers to the outer and the inner, the seen and the unseen, the interlinks within creation and between creation and its Source. Most of the causal links within and between the microcosm and the macrocosm can be investigated and understood. Within the world of the individual we can also easily see the interplay of cause and effect, action and reaction. The same mechanism is at play in the broader workings of the world, and in the relationship between the individual and the world. However, whatever we can rationally discern of the connecting links between all created beings in this world are only aspects of a vaster creational reality. This is because discernment is to do with witnessing and experiencing, functions which necessarily take place within the framework of what has been created. The world of the unseen, the eternal void which was already there before creation, continues within the fabric of experience as we know it, and it is this world that will prevail once all creational form has dissolved.

Life after creation will enter a phase that is subject to neither time nor space. It is therefore not a zone in which we can act or interact. There the self relives the accumulated actions of its previous physical life, having prescribed the experience of the next phase through the intentions and actions of this one. Linking the zones of pre-creation and post-creation, the unicosm includes the present phase of creation in which action and reaction are experienced. The difference between this phase and the next is that here, because of all the mental and egotistical barriers we have placed between ourselves and our deeper reality, we are veiled from seeing the immediacy and truth of that relationship. Like children in a nursery, our concerns and quarrels loom so large that they blot out deeper and more subtle perceptions.

The roots of justice, peace, wisdom and purity all pertain to the world of unicosm. We notice how every action has an equal and opposite reaction, and therefore an ecology of justice and balance is experienced in this world. Human beings are ingrained with a primal and basic code of conduct which enables us to behave according to commonly understandable codes of ethics and morality. We are naturally endowed with the ability to act with reason in order to bring about a certain measure of justice. However, human justice will always be relative. It is only absolute justice that encompasses the seen and the unseen, this world and the next. Absolute or divine justice can only be understood if we add the totality of the inner and outer worlds of a person's experience to that of the world at large (the microcosm and the macrocosm). It is only by casting one's vision along the whole breadth of the spectrum that total justice can be understood, for the world of unicosm engulfs the totality of the seen and the unseen.

The human soul contains a dimension which is beyond time and space (the spirit), and a locus of experience of reality within time and space (the self). If we are truly to experience our universality, or the unicosm within us, we not only need to know the cosmology of the self, we also need to be exposed to the unseen, access to which is gained through a pure trusting heart, in submission to Allah. Access to that state comes with practice and discipline whereby the mind is quietened and all reason and understanding is transcended, until another dimension within the self is awakened to. This state of awareness reflects true elements of creativity which are not tangibly discernible nor motivated by need, desire or any other outward impulse. The pathway to this state is not through acquiring power (such as the so-called paranormal) but through abandoning all powers and will.

The ultimate objective that human beings can achieve in this world is the spontaneous unification between the inner and the outer, the seen and the unseen. As far as the individual is concerned, one experiences the physical limitations and needs of one's biological nature simultaneously with the higher elements and potentials within the self. So while we are able to experience through the senses, we can equally experience an inner dimension that transcends the sensory and therefore the realm of cause and effect.

The world of unicosm is the pinnacle of creational manifestation. Consciousness of the unicosm can be attained by those who have awakened to that in-built potential and who, through discernment and discipline, are ready to be transformed into its higher dimension of reality.

The essence of the Qur'anic and the prophetic teaching is based upon willingness to abandon the world and all attachment to it and, indeed, to experience 'death' before biological death. The Prophet said: 'Die before you die', meaning: transcend all sense and reasoning. The path of Islam does not deny the importance and necessity of reason and care for the physical, for these are vital, primary duties and conditions. But creation is ineluctably driven to discover that other subtle and hidden dimension which can only be unveiled by the death of the senses, by total silence in body, the mind and the inner world. When this happens we are on the threshold of gnosis of a Source that supersedes – in fact, is the cause of – all the power and light in the discernible, measurable world. This Source and Essence is Allah, and all divine attributes emanate from Him.

When this full awakening or gnosis takes place in the individual, a self-governing mechanism simultaneously springs into action. This involves discernment and interaction with the outer world while spontaneously having access to another dimension which always supersedes and guides one's behaviour in this world. The ultimate condition is the realization that although we inhabit the world of reason and duality, the unicosm permeates all the diverse and cyclical appearances of the physical which are forever subject to constant change, emanation and disappearance.

The first step of entry into the world of unicosm is to understand how all actions and manifestations in this world are linked and connected. The next phase in the pilgrim's progress is to arrive at the world of unity of all attributes. Arrival at this sanctum demands that one be willing to sacrifice the most sacred gift of all – life itself. Dying to one's self is to become alive to the world of unity.

3 · THE FUNDAMENTALS OF ISLAM

And [as for] the believing men and the believing women, they
are guardians of each other; they enjoin good and forbid evil
and keep up prayer and pay the poor-rate, and obey Allah and
His apostle; Allah will show mercy to them, surely Allah is
Mighty, Wise.

Qur'an 9:71

Based on self-discipline, Islam provides a complete way of
transacting with oneself and with creation. If the individual
is humble, in submission and in harmony with Allah's decree
– which encapsulates both the visible and invisible worlds –
then his or her behaviour will at all times be constructive and
appropriate. The *Din* or life-transaction of Islam is founded
on the realization of the One God who is the source of all
attributes, actions and creations; that this God is most just
and that this justice will be experienced in this world and the
next; and that creation has come about in order for us to know
God through submission and worship. This knowledge was
most clearly conveyed by the highest of creation, the Prophets
and Messengers, who were the principle receivers of divine
revelation and by those who follow in their path.

The *Din* is based first on acceptance of and submission to
Allah. This is called *islam*. Then follows the application of all
the Islamic teachings so that faith and trust in Allah govern

every action and intention. This step is called *iman*. When *islam* and *iman* have taken hold so that a person behaves and acts in the knowledge that although they do not see God, God sees their every act and intent, then the state of *ihsan* has been reached.

Since the foundation of the *Din* is to acknowledge the One God and that the purpose of this existence is to recognize and obey Him, this is realized through personal and social conduct, worship and other outer practices.

The outer practices of the *Din* of Islam are founded upon the affirmation (*Shahadah*) of the ultimate truth that there is only one God, and that Muhammad is a Prophet of God. After a time this declaration becomes a firm belief, an experienced certainty, and a spiritual 'looking-glass' through which one sees all outer realities in their multiplicity. With this vision the faithful will realize how all these experiences and creations emanate from one source, and that to retain this clear focus one must remain within the prophetic bounds that protect one from confusing and misleading distractions.

Establishing oneself within the arena of the prophetic code of conduct begins with regular, timely acknowledgement of the One and Only All-Encompassing Creator through the practice of prayer (*Salat*). The unique form of this prayer was revealed to the Prophet. *Salat* is to be performed at least five times a day and is regarded as the noblest and supreme act of virtue. The other obligatory acts include alms-giving (*Zakat*), regular fasting (*Sawm*), the obligatory fast being the month of Ramadan, and pilgrimage (*Hajj*). The minimum amounts or percentage of wealth given as *Zakat* are fixed, there being no limit on the maximum amounts. Fasting is a great vigil that purifies the physical body, refines one's higher senses, and deepens sensitivity towards all creation. Pilgrimage is the symbolic act of abandoning the world, returning to it only after having shed all one's desires. The ritual of *Hajj* brings a deep and populous cross-section of humanity together in one spot at a specific time in order to glorify the One Creator.

Other obligatory duties include always doing one's utmost to uphold good and denounce evil, and being willing to strive for and fight in the way of good. This latter act (*Jihad*) includes being ready to lay down one's life for God's cause because life belongs to the Life-giver and we have only been given that power in order to experience this world and return to Source.

THE CREED (SHAHADAH)

The testimony that there is no God but Allah, and that Muhammad is the Messenger of God, begins on the tongue. It is confirmed by the purified and sincere heart until it becomes the pivotal point in one's life, leading to personal transformation. The creed means witnessing that every situation emanates from the One Source and that one is always therefore dependent on that Source for guidance, knowledge, protection and direction.

The proclamation and realization of '*la ilaha illa 'Llah*' (there is no God but Allah) and '*Muhammadun rasulu 'Llah*' (Muhammad is the Messenger of Allah) form the very foundation of the *Din*. From One Essence have come numerous attributes and actions. The path of enlightenment is rooted in the truth that Allah is the Only Source of life, and of all creational manifestation culminating in the human being, who is in potential God's representative in this world.

Thousands of messengers and prophets in different communities, tribes and nations and at different times in history have proclaimed the same reality with appropriate rules and laws governing interactive behaviour. A great many of them came to correct, reinforce or revive what had come before. Dozens of prophets came to the people of Israel to correct and renew the *Din*. Indeed, the Prophet Jesus came to the same people to revive their Islam (then called Judaism), and enhance the inner meaning and purity of that religion which had become heavily burdened by outer ritual, dietary laws and abuse of power by rabbinical figures.

The final seal of all these Messengers is the Prophet Muhammad. According to the Qur'an this message is not for any specific people nor for any specific time or geographical area, but for the posterity of all humanity. This last message of Islam encompasses all other prophetically revealed messages with the fullest dimension of perfected outer laws that can be applied by everyone wherever and whenever.

All vital acts of worship in Islam are based on the Qur'an and the prophetic practices (*Sunnah*), especially those established during the last years of the Prophet's life in Medina. These acts possess numerous understandable benefits as well as more subtle values and meanings. By adhering to all the practices everyone will achieve the degree of enlightenment and gnosis that is attainable according to their understanding of both their human reality and the other divine possibilities.

PRAYER (*SALAT*)

The primary act of worship in Islam is that of prayer. The Qur'an enjoins all the faithful to 'keep up prayer; surely prayer is a timed ordinance for the believers' (4:103). Muslims from earlier days based their prayer on the prophetic practice of five prayers during the three periods of the day: daybreak, noon and mid-afternoon, after sunset and at night. The prayer is preceded by a simple ritual washing (*wudu*), which symbolizes purification of the limbs (actions) and renunciation of any action other than that which is based on the intention to worship and know God.

The *Salat* is performed in a precise order based on three specific postures: standing, bowing and prostrating. These three movements are considered the fundamental pillars of the practice of *Salat*, and each position possesses inner meanings. While one stands in wonderment and adoration, one is calling upon the mercy of God. When one realizes the immensity of divine power one is so awe-struck that one bows in the face of such majesty. And finally one disappears from existence – all that is other than Allah – by prostrating oneself. In prostration one's individual profile and locus of sensory experience (the face) is obliterated in the dust of the earth. As all sensual awareness recedes, inner awareness is enhanced.

The Qur'an describes those who are faithful as being in a perpetual state of *Salat* (70:23). It is not the ritual that is implied here but what the regular ritual imparts in outer action to the person of inner serenity and appropriate orientation.

It is recommended that one should pray in the open air, on

earth and on time. *Salat* is performed facing the Ka'bah in Mecca, the symbolic House of God, which was originally built by Abraham. One is also recommended to pray communally for this has both social and spiritual merit. As a result of this, mosques of all sizes abound in Muslim lands. In the early days of Islam they were ordinary buildings, the same as any other construction, except for the open courtyard ending in a niche that marked the direction of prayer (known as *Qiblah*). Roofs and pillars for structural support, and other architectural and symbolic embellishments, were added later, reflecting local traditions. Once a week on Friday, the day of gathering, there is a larger gathering in the main mosque of every town for the noon prayers, which are preceded by two sermons.

Salat imparts to the individual a re-charge and reaffirmation of faith based on inner stillness and silence contained within specified outer motion. Its social implications are the outer uniformity and equality between all humanity when they face their Creator. Rich and poor, mighty and meek, all stand in obedience and submission to God during their life in this world. It reminds both the individual and society to be humble, inwardly tranquil and content. The individual who performs *Salat* is outwardly and inwardly cleansed. He relinquishes his management of affairs of the world and calls upon the Creator of the Seen and Unseen for guidance and enlightenment. *Salat* is the entryway to knowledge of Allah.

FASTING (SAWM)

O you who believe! Fasting is prescribed for you, as it was for those before you, so that you may guard [against evil].

Qur'an 2:183

Fasting was practised in all those communities which had a Messenger or Prophet. The fasting described in the Qur'an involves abstention from all intake of food or drink from dawn to sunset during one specific month of the year (Ramadan, the ninth month of the Muslim year). The Prophet fasted regularly throughout the year and recommended that all

Muslims should do so. During the last years of his life it is known that he fasted for at least three days of every month.

While keeping the fast it is also necessary to abstain from sexual intercourse as well as any sensory excitement or distraction for one is also recommended to fast with the limbs and sense organs. Fasting also entails not listening to or engaging in slander, refraining from anger and all other vices. One must behave in such a considered way that one acts only to please God.

The benefits of the fast are numerous, ranging from physiological to mental and spiritual benefits, bringing about greater awareness and sensitivity towards oneself and creation.

CHARITY (ZAKAT)

> And keep up the prayer and pay the poor-rate and whatever good you send before yourselves, you shall find it with Allah; surely Allah sees what you do.
>
> Qur'an 2:110

The root of the word *Zakat* means to purify and to increase. Charity or alms-giving is obligatory to every Muslim. Originally *Zakat* was a tax levied on a certain quantity of specified items, such as wheat, barley, dates, raisins, gold, silver and cattle. When a threshold in the quantity of these goods was exceeded then *Zakat* became obligatory.

In the present-day world where most people's income takes the form of money rather than the above-mentioned goods, most Muslims pay the equivalent of around two and a half per cent of their income in *Zakat* as a precaution.

The recipients of *Zakat* are also specified as the poor, the needy, travellers in the way of Allah, and whatever is in the way of Allah and may enhance the *Din*. Many Muslims give *Zakat* to the Imam or *'Alim* (Muslim scholar or jurist) for him to dispense in the best way he knows.

Additional charity and alms-giving is of course encouraged by the Qur'an and *Sunnah*, and there are no set limits. Muslims are enjoined to share whatever they have with others – the Prophet says: 'He is not a Muslim who sleeps in a town where there are hungry people.' In today's world where communication and mobility have created a global village the present equivalent of a town of yesteryear is the whole world. It is therefore the duty of every Muslim to share and care for all humanity, because nowadays we are aware of their plight.

Giving loans (without usury of course) in the way of Allah is another aspect of charity to which no limits are set or obligations imposed except in accordance with one's own conscience and inner upliftment.

PILGRIMAGE (HAJJ)

> And pilgrimage to the House is incumbent upon people for the sake of Allah, [upon] everyone who is able to undertake the journey to it . . .
>
> Qur'an 3:97

The Arabs have performed a ritual pilgrimage around the Ka'bah in the sacred precinct in Mecca from time immemorial. Christians, Jews and many others also brought their offerings and joined in circumambulating the Ka'bah. The Prophet performed the full Islamic Hajj only once and that was during the last year of his life.

Hajj is in two parts: one can be performed at any time of the year (Umrah) and the other includes the stop at Arafat which can only be done on a specific day once a year (Hajj). At a certain distance before entering Mecca the pilgrim performs the ritual ablution and dons the two seamless pieces of white cloth (the Ihram). Having entered the sacred precinct he or she undertakes the prescribed rituals that are so deep in meaning.

The first act is to circle the Ka'bah anti-clockwise seven times. The Ka'bah is a rectangular building which has been rebuilt several times since its initial construction. The sacred Black Stone is embedded in one corner.

Next comes the fast walk between the two hillocks called Safa and Marwa (symbols of caution and hope), relating to the flight of Hagar, the Prophet Abraham's wife, in her search for water for her son Ishmael. One of the inner meanings of this enactment is a replay of what we do every day of our lives – thinking that our desired object of salvation lies somewhere else we constantly run hither and thither.

On the eighth day of the month of *Hajj* the pilgrim must stand on the hill of Arafat a few miles to the east of the Ka'bah from around midday until sunset. Arafat comes from the word meaning 'common knowledge' or 'naturally understandable'. The word in Arabic for 'good deed' is also derived from the same root. Yet another related word is *'irfan*, which means gnosis or knowledge of God. To gather with the mass of humanity on the hills of Arafat, asking for enlightenment and salvation, is the highest act of worship.

After Arafat two further symbolic acts take place at Mina in the desert. The first is to stone the devil in a re-enactment of what Abraham did when an inner voice whispered to him not to sacrifice his son as God had commanded him. The other is to sacrifice an animal as Abraham did when, having resolved to sacrifice his son of desire in the way of the Lord, the ram of his renunciation appeared.

For Muslims all over the world pilgrimage has come to be their central yearly event. The completion of *Hajj* is celebrated on the following day, called the *Eid al-Adha*, *Eid* meaning 'festival' (derived from the root meaning to return, as it returns every year), and *adha* meaning 'sacrifice'.

Apart from the spiritual benefits to the individual, *Hajj* is also a major social, cultural and political market-place of universal proportion. It is here that all Muslims meet, greet, interact and embrace each other. The physical and symbolic point of unity, the Black Stone, witnesses and records their parting kiss.

Hajj has always greatly influenced the life of Muslims for it brings a powerful mass of people together with the express purpose of abandoning this world in pursuit of the knowledge of the Creator of this world. *Hajj* thus links the whole of the Muslim world together. The departure and return of pilgrims is marked with great joy and celebration by their families and communities. Some pilgrims would stay much longer in Mecca and some even chose to settle in the Hejaz and reside in Mecca or Medina, where there can be greater possibilities for studying and meeting prominent men of knowledge. Nowadays of course such freedoms are restricted due to the political sensitivities and controls in Arabia.

STRUGGLE IN THE WAY OF GOOD (*JIHAD*)

Whoever strives hard, he strives only for his own soul; most surely Allah is Self-sufficient, above need of the worlds.

Qur'an 29:6

Striving, struggling and doing one's best in order to achieve a worthy objective are all necessary conditions for human improvement and development. The root word of *Jihad* is derived from the verb meaning to strive, struggle and exert the utmost energy.

Enjoined upon all Muslims, *Jihad* has a hierarchy starting from the Greater *Jihad*, which is against oneself and one's lower tendencies (ranging from lust to greed and all other animalistic inclinations). The Greater *Jihad* is self-purification and inner preparation for the appropriate condition that will lead to correct inspiration and guidance from within – a prelude to greater awakening and enlightenment.

Then there is the striving and struggle in relation to the outer world, which includes helping others, teaching, improving social conditions, and culminating in one's willingness to put one's life in danger when the circumstances demand it:

The believers are only those who believe in Allah and His Apostle, then they doubt not, and struggle hard with their wealth and their lives in the way of Allah; they are the truthful ones.

Qur'an 49:15

It is this act of fighting a war in the way of Allah that has become synonymous in the West with the word *Jihad*. In order to justify *Jihad* in the context of war, Islam enjoins that the cause for such war should be correct and that all other possible courses of action have been exhausted. Only then can *Jihad* of this sort take place. If the very existence of Muslims is in jeopardy and if Muslim leadership is qualified to engage in such an act, then *Jihad* becomes obligatory for those who are able to undertake it.

ENJOINING GOOD AND FORBIDDING EVIL

I swear by Time, Most surely man is in loss, except those who believe and do good and enjoin on each other truth and enjoin on each other patience.

Qur'an 104:1–3

Encouraging goodness and forbidding evil is part of the social fabric and foundation of any civilization. This enjoinder implies that the individual already practising these virtues must remind others and transmit to them this civilized behaviour so that society as a whole may be positively influenced. Decadence and corruption if not checked will always lead to the collapse of society.

4 · The History and Development of the Religion

And thus We have made you a medium [just] nation that you may be the bearers of witness to people and that the Apostle may be a bearer of witness to you . . .

Qur'an 2:143

As Islam spread geographically during the Prophet's life and the next two generations, its fervour and light were so powerfully transformative that it was readily embraced. There was little theological discussion or formulation other than the acceptance of the Qur'an and following the prophetic footsteps in behaviour and practice.

The nature and habits of the people who originally embraced Islam, as well as those who soon followed, were basically simple. Their purity and intact primal qualities were such that when they heard the message of the Qur'an and Islam, they recognized the truth reflected in the teachings. However, as numerous people and nations of entirely different backgrounds, languages and cultures embraced Islam (including a great many Jews, Zoroastrians and others) there emerged a growing number of suspect prophetic traditions and sayings (*Hadith*) that required close scrutiny in order to be authenticated. These needs were the beginnings of the sciences of religion.

Within a hundred years of the Prophet's death records of what he said and did were being made with the name of the persons who transmitted them so as to ensure accurate and reliable chains of human reference. The impact of people coming into Islam from diverse cultures gave rise to numerous theological questions that also addressed their old belief systems. These questions ranged from reincarnation to the nature of hell and paradise, ways of repentance, and so on. The rise of religious scholarship, interpretation and documentation was therefore an unavoidable and natural consequence of the rapid and broad spread of Islam.

Islam was and still is a filter of cultures. Wherever it spread it absorbed a certain coloration from the previous religious culture. Through embracing Islam, converts went through the process of taking on new habits and casting off many redundant past customs. However, there always were and will be some gaps where the filter was not fully applied. The sediment of the past was often reconstituted as though it were acceptable to Islam, a prominent example of this being the oppressive dowry system which, contrary to the original Islamic teachings, often requires the bride's family to supply a dower.

What emerged as Sufism within three hundred of the Prophet Muhammad was basically a renewing and corrective movement to safeguard the essence and spirit of Islam in the face of growing 'establishment' Muslims. Found mostly among Sunnis, the instructional objective of the Sufi networks was to highlight the need for personal purification, constant awareness and self-knowledge, in order to attain gnosis and knowledge of God. A similar stream of Sufi practices called 'Irfan emerged among the Shi'is and other minority sects.

In the first six to seven centuries of Islam Muslim rulership and institutions became more established and entrenched, giving rise to conventional patterns of Muslim behaviour which became the status quo.

FIRST-CENTURY MUSLIMS

Most of the Prophet's companions spared no effort to master the *Din* of Islam. During the last two years of his life several hundred people had memorized the Qur'an and many more could quote numerous prophetic sayings and traditions.

The importance of language for the Arabs was such that the highest merit and prestige was attached to memorizing and repeating the prophetic teaching in its original form. It was a matter of pride for the Companions and those following them to be able to quote the appropriate verse of the Qur'an or a tradition in order to clarify a certain issue of behaviour or a matter of worship.

The light of the Prophet's transmission was such that most people who came into contact with him would be saturated by the clarity of his message and the radiance of his presence. Those who came to him with doubts and questions found their uncertainties exchanged for confirmation and confidence. Many of these people were transformed by their commitment to Islam, and it was this transformative element in Islam that engendered the rapid growth and spread of the *Din*.

It is reasonable to say that during the first century there was little social distinction between the *Ulama* (scholars), Qur'an experts, jurists and the common people. Everyone was expected to know their *Din* to the fullest possible extent. For the early generation of Companions it was enlightenment that mattered. Learning and applying the *Din* was necessary for their transformation. The tradition of analytical study, or what we now call education, did not exist in a formal format of isolating topics and subjecting them to discourse and argument. The Qur'an and the *Sunnah* were not talked about so much as lived.

The way that the people of Medina (most of whom were Companions of the Prophet) acted and interacted during the time of 'Umar (the peak in early Muslim dynamic and creative spread) was to become the model towards which most Muslims look as epitomizing the ideal committed community. The close Companions of the Prophet acted according to their knowledge of the Qur'an and their familiarity with the behavioural standards he established. Minor differences in interpretation did not cause major divergences, partly because events outside Medina were moving so rapidly and Muslims soon found themselves sucked into the vacuum left by the collapse of the Byzantine and Sassanian Empires.

Great teachers of this living path emerged in different parts of Muslim lands, in particular the non-Arab ones. They in turn became the conduits for strains of specialization in the propounding of knowledge. One such teacher was Hasan Al-Basri, considered by most Sufis to be the first Sufi, and to whom is attributed the emergence of the *Mu'tazilis* (literally, 'those who keep themselves apart from dispute'). The general belief of the *Mu'tazilis* was that truth could be reached by applying reason to what was revealed in the Qur'an, thereby arriving at answers. They held that God was just and had no human attributes and that the Qur'an must have been created in some special way by Him. The teachings of Hasan al-Basri and the great Companions such as Abu Dharr, Ibn 'Abbas and Imam 'Ali were used by later scholars to elucidate and illustrate some of the vaguer points in the Qur'an or *Sunnah*.

Many Jews and Christians who embraced Islam in the last years of the Prophet's life and during the following generations brought with them practices and traditions which they felt were complementary to Islamic life. Upon further scrutiny, later Muslim scholars uncovered the doubtfulness of many such 'imported' traditions (as they had become attributed to the Prophet). These were later labelled *isra'iliyat* (a plural noun meaning 'from the people of Israel').

The outward geographical thrust of the message of Islam mirrored the vibrant waves of inner transformation generated by the Prophet. The dialectical discourses on matters and social ramifications of faith that developed came to be known as the science of *Kalam* (literally, 'speech'). Questions regarding free will and predestination and other ideological, metaphysical, philosophical and speculative issues only began to be systematically addressed after the second and third generations of Muslims. It was not until the middle of the second Islamic century that distinctive thinkers and schools of thought in theology and law took clear definition.

Gathering and Recording the Teachings

From the early days after the Prophet, Muslims began to study and interpret the Qur'an and prophetic way (*Sunnah*). Traditions (*Hadith*) which recorded what the Prophet said and did were collected, memorized and referred to as source material for the basic obligations of Muslims, which came to be called the Pillars of Islam (see Chapter 1).

THE QUR'AN

> This is the Book; there is no doubt in it, a guide for those who are precautiously aware.
>
> Qur'an 2:2

When the Prophet died there were known to have been at least seven different readings of the Qur'an in the main tribal or regional dialects. By the time of the third Caliph ('Uthman) the territorial spread and cultural diversity of the converts – speaking dozens of new languages – made it clear that the tolerance for different dialects shown in the early days could no longer continue. During 'Uthman's caliphate it was decided to standardize the language of the Qur'an according to the dominant language of the Quraysh. Several copies of the Hafs version (a copy of the Qur'an in the keeping of one of the Prophet's wives) were therefore made and distributed to Egypt, Syria and Iraq. The Quraysh Arabic version thus became the universal standard, imparting a certain prestige on to the people of Quraysh.

The Qur'an needed to be explained both to the common Muslim and to the new converts. The Meccan revelations – focusing on nature, Allah and the universe – require a certain spiritual and metaphysical preparation to understand. Besides their universal applicability, the Medina revelations were a stream of teaching, grooming and guidance for the early community. Certain injunctions superseded earlier ones, though the latter remained part of the Qur'an. For example, soon after it was revealed that prayer was not to be performed while drunk (4:43), alcohol was forbidden altogether (5:90–91).

Exposition of the Qur'an was and is also necessary because the meaning of certain words has changed and evolved subsequent to the revelation. For example, at the time of the Prophet *fiqh* meant deep inner understanding and a practitioner of *fiqh* (a *faqih*) was someone possessed of such understanding, particularly in the context of being able to divine how many months pregnant a camel was. Two centuries later *fiqh* came exclusively to mean jurisprudential reasoning.

Famous Qur'anic interpretations include those of Al-Mahalli (d.864), Al-Tabari (d.923), Az-Zamakhshari (d.1144), a Mu'tazili, and Al-Baydawi (d.1282) whose commentary was used as the standard text in traditional courses. These commentaries were based on oral traditions of the Prophet and his Companions, in particular of his nephew 'Abdullah Ibn Al-'Abbas.

Shi'i scholars such as 'Ayyashi and Tabarsi also wrote commentaries, and the Sufi commentaries of Ibn 'Arabi and al-Kashani are still popular and available. Ar-Razi (d.1209) wrote an Ash'ari commentary (see pages 57–8 for an explanation of Ash'ari thought). Thus Qur'anic study became part of the science of the 'roots' of the *Din*.

HADITH

> They desire to put out the light of Allah with their mouths, but Allah will perfect His light, even though the disbelievers may be averse.
>
> Qur'an 61:8

With the skills of accurate memorization so deeply ingrained in Arab culture, many of the Prophet's Companions committed his sayings to memory and passed them on to other converts. The Prophet himself ensured that his own utterances were kept distinct from the Qur'an and from those sayings that were inspired directly by Allah (called *Hadith Qudsi*, sacred or divine tradition).

With the advent of dynastic rule in Damascus within fifty years of *Hijrah*, a certain number of fabricated, erroneous traditions began to circulate (sometimes to justify the more dubious actions of the ruling élite). Prophetic justice and conduct as practised by Muhammad and the early Caliphs and Companions were sometimes replaced by arbitrary and often inhuman and cruel ways by the Arab rulers of Damascus (only to be surpassed later by the Abbasid rulers of Baghdad). The services of friendly but corrupt narrators of tradition and 'Ulama were used to find traditions which, if taken out of context, could justify the means to their ends. The Prophet had however warned against 'Ulama knocking at the palace doors of rulers, and furthermore he had actually praised the ruler who could be found at the door of an 'Alim. The Muslim masses came contemptuously to recognize such disgraced 'Ulama as the 'Palace 'Ulama'.

Such abuse did not detract from the fact that sincere seekers of knowledge travelled far and wide in order to select and scrutinize traditions and authenticate their chains of transmission. This process of investigation became the science of Hadith in which the correctness and soundness of a tradition was gauged by the qualities of the men and women (their piety, truthfulness, knowledge of language etc.) forming the links in the chains of transmission. Later on the Hadith scholars began to classify them according to their reliability, and produced numerous collections which subsequently became major works of reference for all Muslims.

The science of Hadith burgeoned during the second and third Islamic centuries, but it was not until the ninth century CE that several large collections appeared, the most famous of which are those of Bukhari (d. 870) and Muslim (d. 875), both Sunnis. The Shi'is collected their traditions from their Imams, appointed from among the descendants of the Prophet's family, who relayed them from the Prophet.

The most famous Sunni collections of Hadith are popularly referred to as the 'Six Books', the two most authoritative of which are those already mentioned. The other collections are those of Abu Dawud (d.875), Tirmidhi (d.892), An-Nasa'i (d.915) and Ibn Maja (d.886). The Shi'is based their collections on 'Four Books', which subsequently appeared as several large collections, none of which claims absolute authority as the Sunnis do for theirs. This is because while the majority of Hadith are considered authentic, there are always a few in each collection that are suspect.

Actual transmission of religious learning was often done man to man, in or around a mosque. A teacher of the Qur'an or *Hadith* would sit in one corner of the mosque while students gathered around him, several of whom would eventually become teachers themselves. Popular teachers were sought out by advanced students, wherever they were. Scholastic specialization and earning one's keep from such teaching was not customary until much later. Indeed, it was (and remains) disapproved of to charge people for teaching them the Qur'an and the *Din*.

As the role of mosques in the community developed and grew in importance, they also became the centres of religious colleges. Each important city built a major Friday Mosque as well as a seminary (*madrasah*). The most famous and extensive seminary, the Nizamiyah, was built in Baghdad in the eleventh century CE, by the first Seljuk ruler's vizier, Nizam Al-Mulk (after whom it was named). One of the Nizamiyah's principal teachers was Imam Ghazali. A typical *madrasah* would have several halls (called *diwans*) opening on to a central courtyard, each one used by a teacher for a certain period of time. Some of these halls became known for a specific type of teaching. This architectural layout later found its way through Muslim Andalusia to Europe to become the cloisters of Western Christian theological schools and Oxbridge universities.

Most of these seminaries were endowed with a trust (*waqf*) providing the funds needed for its upkeep and operation. Sometimes these endowments came from the rental of shops or buildings attached to the mosque of the *madrasah*. Some *madrasahs* later came to specialize in one of the Schools of Thought or Jurisprudence (*madhhab*). The numerous Muslim judges and *Muftis* as well as the simple Imam of local mosques were often associated with a particular *madrasah*.

The curriculum of such *madrasahs* covered the Arabic language, logic, the Qur'an (often memorized in its entirety), annals of the early period of Islam, the science of reciting and interpreting the Qur'an and *Hadith*, the basis and roots of religious belief, jurisprudence and law (*fiqh*), and ritual worship. With minor variations the main topics and methods of teaching continue to the present day in most *madrasahs* across the Muslim world.

When a student mastered a certain level of teaching, he would be given a licence and certificate testifying completion of the course. Eventually the senior student would reach a point where he himself could teach until he became a full jurist. From these *madrasahs* there emerged thousands of variously ranked Muslim teachers, clerics and great jurist-consults.

SCHOOLS OF LAW

By the end of the seventh century CE it had already become the standard practice for the ruler or governor to appoint special scholars (called *Qadis*) to dispense justice. To exercise such judgements the *Qadi* needed to know the Qur'an and the prophetic teachings, as well as the cumulative practice of the laws of earlier communities.

As Islam spread, local cultural habits and practices had to be taken into consideration. Whenever the Islamic teachings did not contradict or negate local custom it was allowed to continue. Growing concern with doctrinal matters led to the development of various lines of thought and consideration of the prophetic teachings. The need for consensus among Muslims in matters of practical jurisprudence soon began to loom large. From around the middle of the eighth century CE, and upon the creation of a centralized bureaucratic state (see pages 79–84), it became essential for rulers to accept that whatever was agreed upon should be seen to be based upon the teachings of Islam. The very nature of centralized government demanded general agreement about the practical implications of Islamic rule. The Qur'an, *Sunnah*, *Hadith* and the opinion of scholars, as well as the permitted customary practices of local communities, formed the basis upon which judgement was to be made.

In assessing new situations that demanded rulings, the learned Muslim or jurist used the mechanism of analogy (*Qiyas*) while at the same time exercising reason in order to arrive at appropriate answers that were not explicit in the Qur'an and *Sunnah*. The idea was to try to find an element in the present situation which was similar, in a relevant way, to an element in a past situation on which a ruling had already been made. Such a disciplined exercise of reason came to be know as *ijtihad* (literally, 'utmost effort), for our purposes, jurisprudence. This process of *ijtihad* was justified by *Hadith* that encouraged learning and the learned to pass on their knowledge ('the learned are the heirs of the Prophet'). When there was a general agreement as a result of such an exercise of reason then the consensus (*ijma'*) would be accorded the status of unquestionable truth. *Ijma'* was later defined as the consensus of scholars whose competence and piety were incontestable. In all of this, knowledge of Arabic was considered essential.

Based upon these accepted principles and the process of thought that developed, a body of law emerged, called *fiqh*, the applied product of which later came to be know as the *Shari'ah*. Gradually over a period of about two centuries, a number of schools each known as a *madhhab* grew out of such practice. Each *madhhab* eventually took its name from the main scholar from whom it originated, such as the Hanafi from Abu Hanifa and the Maliki from Malik Ibn Anas. During their lifetimes these scholars were just teachers, albeit pre-eminent ones, for scholarship was very much open to all. A natural historical process of selection brought the five present-day major schools of thought into acceptance by the establishment.

Abu Hanifa (699–767) placed the emphasis on opinions reached by individual reasoning, and used analogy extensively. His broad interpretations displayed a flexibility that increased the appeal of his jurisprudence, particularly to rulers who sought easy justifications for their actions. He was by profession a trader in silk in Kufa, where he also taught, and the school of law that now bears his name claims the largest number of Sunni adherents.

Malik (715–795) worked on the assumption that the ways of the elders of Medina (the Companions of the Prophet and their descendants) should be uncorrupted either by the new converts or tribal ways, or by the influence of the subsequently developed garrison towns. The practice of Medina was the way of Muhammad and from this an idealized model of Medina emerged.

It was Al-Shafi'i (767–820) who brought greater clarity to the different bases for legal decisions. He regarded of paramount importance all the general principles as well as the specific commandments in the Qur'an. Equally important were the prophetic practices recorded in the *Hadith*, which he regarded as more important than the cumulative practices of the communities. For him the way of the Prophet was the manifestation of God's will, amply confirming or elaborating on the Qur'anic injunctions. The words and deeds of the Prophet drew out the implications and provisions of the Qur'an, and thus the *Sunnah* complemented the Qur'an.

Ibn Hanbal (d.855), to whom the Hanbali school is attributed, used the foundation of Al-Shafi'i for the development of his line of thought. He emphasized methods of choosing *Hadith*, even preferring a weak *Hadith* over a strong analogy.

The principles of legal reasoning (the roots of *fiqh*) grew into an important arena of scholarship as they dealt with the place of *Hadith* and the legitimacy of such traditions, as well as the limits and method of *ijtihad*. Shi'i Muslim groups developed their own system of law and moral precepts, which came to be called the Ja'fari school of law, so named after its foremost exponent, the sixth Shi'i Imam Ja'far As-Sadiq (d.765) who was the greatest teacher of his time in Medina. Both Abu Hanifa and Imam Malik were among those, said to number four thousand, who benefited from his teachings. Ja'fari *fiqh* regarded consensus as valid only if the opinion of the Imam was included. The line of development in Shi'i jurisprudence was more direct because of the belief that the Imams were infallible. The Imams simply reflected and therefore reproduced the original prophetic teaching in different circumstances over a period of time. As a result of this advantage, they did not need to resort to analogy (which indeed later became unacceptable in Shi'i theology) nor was much importance attached to consensus. They considered 'Ali and the Ahl al-Bayt (the household of the Prophet) to be the best interpreters of the Qur'an and prophetic teachings. Thus the Shi'i school is based entirely on traditions and teachings from the twelve Imams, each of whom was appointed by his predecessor, starting from 'Ali Ibn Abi Talib and therefore the Prophet himself. The last Imam entered occultation, and his return is awaited as the saviour.

It was not until almost the tenth century CE that the five

main Schools of Law (Hanafi, Maliki, Shafi'i, Hanbali and Shi'i or Ja'fari) became accepted by Muslim rulers as well as the Muslim public. Towards the end of the ninth century, the *Ulama* had come to occupy the most important position in state and society as the guardians of Islam. The public expected their *Ulama* to set the limits and censure the rulers if necessary. Popular *Ulama* often acted as spokesmen and representatives of their communities. It was around this time that it also became a tradition for the great *Ulama* to keep themselves apart from both government and society in order to preserve an independent foundation for the guidance of the community.

It is a sad historical fact that all the masters of *fiqh* and founders of the main surviving Schools were persecuted to varying degrees by the governments of their day. Abu Hanifa, Imam Malik, Ibn Hanbal and Imam Ja'far As-Sadiq in particular suffered greatly and were brutally victimized by their contemporary rulers. From as early as the Damascus caliphate under the Marwani clan (characterized by a nepotistic and decadent amalgam of an Islamicized, Byzantine style of rule), the rulers managed to attract weak and pliant *Ulama* to their courts, and this practice continued throughout Muslim history, thus creating a gap between the rulers and the ruled. In spite of human mischief, however, the spirit of Islam was preserved, leaving the door open in every age for the renewal and purification of the *Din*.

THEOLOGY AND PHILOSOPHY

While the teaching of *fiqh* developed in the arena of mosques and *madrasahs*, serious and profound enquiry in theology and philosophy developed alongside it. New issues begged new solutions, and in response to the debate among scholars and thinkers a framework of theology and philosophical enquiry gradually evolved. Crucial issues such as predestination versus free will, the nature of the Qur'anic text (whether it was a creation of God in essence only or in sound and letters), and others pertaining to reincarnation and the hereafter were debated, and the methodology used gave rise to the science of dialectical theology or *Kalam*.

Dialectical theology originated during the latter part of the first century of Islam. It had begun with the study of the tenets of religious belief, from which developed the Mu'tazili teaching of applying reason and dialectical speculation to all matters religious and philosophical. In employing the rationalistic philosophical approach, the Mu'tazili teachings became the source for subsequent theologians. By the eleventh century CE, however, Mu'tazili teaching was suppressed in Baghdad and elsewhere under the influence of the Abbasid caliphs and Seljuq rulers. *Kalam* nevertheless remained an important aspect of Shi'i theology (see pages 58–62), but in the Sunni world it was overtaken by Ash'ari thought.

Originally a Mu'tazili, Al-Ash'ari (d.935) had abandoned their rationalism to make space for the transcendency of God (which meant that ultimately piety was not an automatic guarantee of entry into heaven), though he retained their dialectical methodology which came to form the basis for Sunni dogma. It was mainly the traditionalist teachings of Ibn Hanbal that emphasized *Hadith* and the Qur'an as the basis on which *fiqh* could rest. He opposed *Kalam*, as did some of the Shafi'is, while the dominant Maliki school discouraged all theological speculation.

Imam Ghazali (d.1111), a Persian master of Ash'ari *Kalam*, tried to reconcile the Ash'ari thinking with that of the Mu'tazili. He held that discursive reason and argument should be used to defend right belief derived from the Qur'an and *Hadith* against those who denied it. It was at best, therefore, a defensive activity. Imam Ghazali's chief work concerned the intimate relationship between observing Islamic law and theology, and their higher meaning, and during his latter years he immersed himself in what he refers to as *ma'rifah* (gnosis) or Sufism.

Imam Ghazali criticized the philosophers, accusing them that their God was not the God of the Qur'an. This challenge was later met by Ibn Rushd (Averroes), the Andalusian philosopher, who justified philosophical debate by referring to the Qur'an: 'Have they not considered the dominions of the Heavens and what things God created?' He showed the harmonious continuity between the prophetic revelations and the conclusions of the great philosophers.

Central to Islamic philosophical enquiry was the assumption that human reason would ultimately lead to the attainment of truth, which could be demonstrated by the first men in this line of thought such as Al-Kindi, Al-Farabi and Ibn Sina (Avicenna). Ibn Sina articulated the truth of Islam according to Aristotelian logic and Greek metaphysics which he had studied thoroughly.

By the twelfth century there was a significant rapprochement between dialectical theology and philosophy, from which there emerged a logical structure to explain the revelations of the Qur'an. In his writings about the stages and experiences of those who embark upon the path of awakening, Avicenna refers to the radiation of Divine Light, by which man is able to attain higher unveilings. For his pains, Al-Suhrawardi, a Persian philosopher who had further formulated such theosophical ideas, was executed in Aleppo in 1191 by the orthodoxy. It was the great metaphysical teacher Ibn 'Arabi (d.1240) of Andalus who formulated a detailed vision of the universe as an endless flow of existence from and returning to the Divine Creator. He explained the unity of being, that all created beings were manifestations of particular Names (that is, attributes) of God through the mediation of images, while human beings were capable of manifesting all these realities. The idea of the perfect, complete man that was put forward by Ibn 'Arabi was later expounded upon by Al-Jili (d.1417).

The philosophers, in particular Ibn 'Arabi, drew considerable criticism from the conventional *Ulama*, especially from Ibn Taymiyah, a zealous Damascene scholar whose literalist interpretations form the bedrock of Wahhabi doctrine (see page 65). He argued along the conventional line that man was not a manifestation of Divine Light and the only way he could draw near to God was by simple and literal obedience to God's commands.

SUNNI-SHI'I RELATIONSHIPS

One of the most important socio-political issues in life is that of leadership, its quality, authority and method of appointment. The Qur'an and the prophetic teachings emphasize obedience to Allah, His Prophet and the upright 'people of authority'.

No Muslim disagrees with this. It is only with the method of legitimizing a 'person of authority' that differences occur and around which the Sunni and Shi'i theologies diverge.

During the early centuries of Islam the terms *Sunni* and *Shi'i* meant different things at different times, as did many other names designating various schools of thought. It was not until the eleventh and twelfth centuries that the current pattern of usage stabilized.

Sunni essentially means one who follows the *Sunnah*, which is the desired aim of every sincere Muslim. It has come to mean, however, those Muslims who follow the *Sunnah* and *Jama'ah*, that is, the way of Muhammad and the consensual majority of Muslims. The term was first adopted by a faction of Muslims who had accepted Abbasid rule, stressing the importance of its continuity with the Marwani past. It was well over a century after Muhammad that the term *Sunni* began to be widely used to distinguish between the largest common group (which is the literal meaning of *Jama'ah*) and the Shi'i, that is, those who were loyal to 'Ali's party. It also implied those who strictly and exclusively referred to the *Hadith* as opposed to engaging in theological and philosophical discourse as a means of gaining guidance. In latter-day usage Sunni has become synonymous with 'orthodox', though it would be more accurate to employ the term Jama'ah to signify the popular mainstream.

In the early years after the Prophet's death the term *Shi'i* meant 'follower' or 'partisan', with particular reference to 'Ali. The Shi'is believe that the Prophet had categorically appointed 'Ali Ibn Abi Talib as his successor at the gathering of Ghadir Khum. 'Ali in turn nominated as his successor his eldest son Hasan, who then nominated his brother Husayn and so on through another ten generations of the Prophet's descendants. Although the Sunnis all acknowledge the event at Ghadir Khum, they take the Prophet's message as merely an acknowledgement of 'Ali's merit rather than a definite political appointment.

In the end, however, the successor to the Prophet was elected by a group of Medinan elders (while the Prophet was being buried). The first Muslim ruler (later to be called Caliph) was Abu Bakr, the Prophet's father-in-law and a close and loyal Companion. Though 'Ali and his followers made occasional protests, they did not contest or revolt against the early Caliphs. 'Ali himself remained loyal to the cause of Islam and served wherever and whenever he could alongside his predecessors. Upon the demise of the third Caliph, however, 'Ali was elected the fourth.

After 'Ali's assassination, Mu'awiyah of the Bani Umayyah took over and moved the seat of political power to Damascus. There he introduced a dynastic and personalized style of despotic rule, with flagrant disregard for the teachings of the Qur'an and Muhammad. His takeover resulted in increased agitation among many of the more pious and committed Muslims (including some Companions and first generation Muslims) in Mecca, Medina and elsewhere. Their legitimate protests were retrospectively labelled as the 'second affliction' by historians, the first being the murder of the Caliph 'Uthman.

The rise of Imam Husayn (the saintly grandson of the Prophet) and his martyrdom in Karbala was the ultimate protest against the imperial rule of Damascus, and marks a turning point in the history of the Muslims. He was regarded by the Shi'is and other sympathizers as the third legitimate successor to the Prophet. His murder was therefore considered to be the ultimate betrayal of Islam and those most qualified to lead Muslims.

The general Sunni stance on leadership was that peace under an unjust ruler was better than anarchy under a just one. For the Shi'i, justice in the government of human affairs could not grow if the ruler did not reflect the Prophet. The ruler had the status of a prophetic figure who, in the Prophet's absence, should be the ultimate spiritual and temporal authority. The prophetic mantle was taken up by the Sufis in the person of their *Shaykhs* or teachers. This fact is significant because while most Sufis were Sunni, the necessity for enlightened leadership reflects the essential nature of transmission of knowledge and guidance. Hence the Shi'is turned to their Imams.

The Shi'i belief in the Imam stems from various interpretations of the Qur'an and traditions which indicate that God in His wisdom and justice would not leave people unguided at any time. The Prophet is reported to have said that there would be twelve just rulers and caliphs after him, the last of whom would go into occultation and would reappear at a time when the world would be engulfed in darkness and injustice to renew the Din and establish justice. The Imams' lives were marked by great piety and service to the community, transmitting their knowledge to those around them and maintaining wherever possible a distance from their contemporary ruling classes who often persecuted them and caused their deaths.

During the tenth and eleventh centuries CE when many Shi'is ruled in different parts of the Muslim world, considerable collections of traditions were made and the foundations laid for the future Shi'i theology. Eventually the mainstream of the Shi'i school of thought became known as the Ithna 'Ashari, the Twelver or Ja'fari (these terms are interchangeable) school of law. The Zaidis were an early offshoot of the Shi'i school who flourished and survived in several parts of the Middle East, mainly in the Yemen.

Throughout the history of the Muslims there have been many Shi'i uprisings, most of them crushed by the authorities. However many Shi'i principalities and kingdoms existed and Shi'is ruled indirectly especially during in the eleventh century CE. This is discussed further in Chapter 5.

By the thirteenth century a cohesive fiqh emerged based on ijtihad. Collections of Hadith narrated through the Imams were established, and the Mujtahids (practitioners of ijtihad) had become the focal point for pious Shi'is, as the majority of them had come to reject the Sunni ruling establishment of their day. Among the early great Shi'i scholars was Al-Mufid (945–1022), who was considered one of the fathers of Kalam. Al-Murtada (966–1044) greatly influenced the Shi'is by giving prominence to the role of the intellect and the process of reasoning. During the thirteenth and fourteenth centuries jurisprudence was fully developed by Al-Muhaqqiq (1205–1277) and Allama Al-Hilli (1250–1325), whose works were subsequently elaborated by Makki Al-Amili (1333–1384). Later on the collection entitled Al Kafi by Kulayni became accepted as the most important collection of Hadith for Shi'is.

While Shi'is accepted only those traditions that were transmitted through their Imams, those Sunni Hadith which did not contradict them were also accepted. Communal consensus, however, had no place in Shi'i theology unless it carried the consensus of the community around the Imam. In Shi'i theology unlike Sunni theology, the exercise of reason replaced consensus as an important instrument for developing law.

Other differences between Shi'i and Sunni law relate to minor aspects of worship and *fiqh*, such as rules of inheritance and temporary marriage (which was lawful during the Prophet's time but made unlawful during that of 'Umar). Ironically, when taken all together, these differences are no greater (and are in many cases even fewer) than those that exist between the various Sunni schools of thought themselves.

Political confrontation between the two reached a peak during the Safavid and Ottoman Empires. However, the nineteenth and twentieth centuries have seen great efforts made by prominent *'Ulama* to bring Shi'is and Sunnis together by encouraging rational dialogue and mutual understanding in place of the popularized emotion that has often been roused by external enemies to divide Muslims.

The success or failure of these rapprochements has depended to a large extent on the private attitudes and political expediencies of the rulers on both sides. It is important to note, however, that love for the Prophet and his household, and reverence for them as great saintly beings, was felt throughout Muslim societies everywhere. Even in the extreme north-west of Africa in what is now Morocco, rulers and kings took overt pride in being descendants of the Prophet's family, a claim which has also been made by others such as the monarchy of Jordan to further legitimize their rule in the eyes of the Muslim masses. To this day the ability to trace one's ancestry to the Prophet carries great prestige among all Muslims, rich and poor alike.

PROMINENT SECTS

ISMA'ILIS

The Ismai'lis came into being after the death of Imam Ja'far As-Sadiq in 765, the sixth Shi'i Imam or spiritual successor to the Prophet. Ja'far's eldest son Isma'il had died while his father was still alive but in spite of that he was held to be his successor by a minority of adherents who later took on his name.

Isma'ili doctrine, which was formulated in the late eighth and early ninth centuries, stresses the dual nature of Qur'anic interpretation, the exoteric and the esoteric. The Isma'ili organization is hierarchical with an Imam as head 'missionary'.

The first Isma'ili caliphate was established in Tunis in 909 by Ubayd Allah who claimed descent from the Prophet Muhammad through Fatima, his daughter, from which they took their dynastic name of Fatimid. Having conquered Egypt in 969 they created a widespread missionary network with followers all over the Islamic world.

The Isma'ilis failed to agree on who should succeed the Fatimid Caliph Al-Mustansir (d.1094). His son Al-Musta'li was recognized in Egypt, but in Syria and Iran his elder son Nizar was claimed for succession, thus creating two eponymous branches.

When the last Fatimid Caliph was deposed by Saladin in 1171 Isma'ili rule in Egypt ended. The Musta'li Isma'ilis survived in Yemen, and in the sixteenth century the leading Musta'li relocated to Gujurat in India, where they are now known as Bohras.

NIZARIS

The Nizaris survived and split into two rival groups, one of which lasted through to the eighteenth century, while the other, headed by the Agha Khan, moved from Iran to India in 1841 after an unsuccessful rebellion. The Agha Khanate's main following is in India and Pakistan and in parts of Iran, Africa and Syria.

BOHRAS

Estimated to number over a million today, the Bohras were originally a Hindu caste who became Musta'li Isma'ili Muslims. They do not recognize the Agha Khan as their spiritual leader, but follow instead an absolute preacher (*Da'i Mutlaq*), resident in their centre in Bombay. With centres in Gujurat and East Africa, they are by inclination traders, which their name incidentally implies, for in Gujurati *vahauru* means to trade.

DRUZE

The Druze sect sprang from the agitations of the Qarmatians (who were Muslims) towards the Fatimids in the eleventh century. A relatively small Middle Eastern sect, it originated in Cairo and was initially developed by a Turk called Muhammad Ad-Darazi. Its members have figured prominently in history, particularly in the wars against the Crusaders. Characterized by secretive doctrines focused around messianism, incarnation and cohesive loyalty among its members, the Druze permit no conversion and no inter-marriage, and allow the practice of *taqiyyah* which permits them to outwardly conform to the mores of any group among whom they find themselves.

ALAWIS

The Alawis, who number 2–3 million, constitute a minority sect of Shi'is found mostly in Syria, where their greatest influence was in Aleppo. They have become politically dominant since 1971 when they took control in the country, but in the past they were persecuted and marginalized by the Crusaders, Mamluks and Ottomans after the fall of Shi'i rule. Their doctrines came from the teachings of Muhammad Ibn Nusayr An-Namari (850), a contemporary of the tenth Shi'i Imam, Ali Al-Hadi, but were established by Husayn Ibn Hamdan Al-Khasibi (d.957) during the Hamdanid dynasty (905–1004). The Alawis accept the pillars of Islamic belief as symbolic but not binding.

BAHA'IS

The founder of the Baha'i sect, the self-named Baha' Allah (1817–1892), declared himself 'The Promised One' of the Bab, a charismatic mystic who had prophesied the advent of a Messiah. The Baha'is were an offshoot of the Babi sect in Persia, which was to some degree an offshoot of the Shaykhis who had broken away from the Shi'i mainstream. In 1863 the Persian government, wanting to rid itself of both parties, requested the Ottomans to imprison their leaders, who were subsequently exiled to Cyprus and to Acre in Palestine. Baha' Allah was buried in Haifa, where his shrine is much visited by Baha'is who are active in Europe, America and Iran (though they have encountered persecution there since the Islamic revolution). Baha'is emphasize brotherly love and world peace and do not possess much religious dogma or ritual.

WAHHABIS

Now dominant in Saudi Arabia and Qatar, the Wahhabis gained a foothold in India, Africa and elsewhere at the beginning of the nineteenth century. The founder, Muhammad Ibn 'Abd Al-Wahhab (1703– 1792), based his teachings on the Hanbali school of law and one of its prominent promoters, Ibn Taymiyah. He was born in a poor village in Arabia, studied in Medina and travelled in Iran and Iraq. He eventually established his austere doctrine in the village of Dir'iyyah in the Najd desert, where it was well received by the Emir Muhammad Ibn Sa'ud, whose daughter he married. In 1802 the Wahhabis captured and ransacked Karbala and seized Mecca in 1803, eventually taking control over the Najd from the Turks. The Sa'uds were driven out of Riyadh by the Egyptian ruler Muhammad 'Ali in 1891 but it was recaptured in 1901 by the young Abd Al-'Aziz Al-Sa'ud, and from there with material and political help from Britain, his kingdom grew to include the desert country of Saudi Arabia, becoming a major supplier of oil to the industrialized world under US protection.

The rigid Wahhabi doctrine has in a sense become its own school of law since its adherents are know for their policy of compelling their followers and other Muslims to observe the formal and ritualistic duties of Islam, denying all aspects of inner awakening, gnosis or enlightenment.

AHMADIS

The Ahmadiyyah movement or sect was founded by Mirza Ghulam Ahmad (1835–1908), a Sunni from the Punjab, who initially reacted against Christian missionaries and the West's political and economic colonialism. He did not, however, instigate *Jihad* as a course of action, but instead advocated awaiting the 'awakening' of the Islamic world. After his death his followers split into two groups, the Qadianis and the Lahoris. The former regard him as a latter-day Prophet, while the latter hold that he was a renewer of the faith. Both parties were energetic in their proselytizing, establishing mosques and publishing propaganda material and have communities in America, Europe, Pakistan and West Africa.

SUFISM AND ENLIGHTENMENT

Sufism or *tasawwuf* most probably derives its name from either the word *suf*, meaning wool, which was used to make the modest robes worn by the early Companions of the Prophet, or from the root word *safa*, meaning purity. It is sometimes referred to as Islamic mysticism and the heart or spirit of Islam.

The Prophet's life and that of many of his Companions and those who followed him was based on a unified cosmology of being. They saw the interconnectedness of the seen and the unseen, the outer and the inner, reason and beyond reason. No Muslim sought a 'mystical' way of life *per se*. What they sought was the Essence and Source of creation. If there were any mystery or mystical aspects to life, they were to be left as such, until they were unveiled from the unseen. The duty of humankind was to concern themselves with what was existentially important and remain in a constant state of awareness, submission to and love for the Creator.

The teachings of the Sufis derive from the Qur'an and *Sunnah*. The Qur'an constantly warns against accumulation in this world and attachment to worldly possessions. Allah reminds humanity to reflect and meditate upon the natural world and the transient nature of all forms of existence. We are encouraged to visit the ruins of past great civilizations to reflect upon what is left of their greatness. Remembrance of the next life and preferring it to this life is repeatedly enjoined in the Qur'an.

The qualities of personal piety, perpetual remembrance,

prayer and abandonment that formed the basis of Islam were all the more focused on by the Sufis through example. The Caliph 'Umar was known to have had no possessions other than what was in his immediate use. He often slept in the mosque, with a mud brick under his head. Salman Al-Farsi was at that time appointed governor of a province but his only possession was a small vessel from which to drink water. The majority of the first and second generation Muslims lived a life of piety, outer asceticism, generosity, courage, inner purity and light.

By the end of the first century we find Muslim rulers mostly concerned with governing, acquiring and establishing dynastic rule and, in many instances, emulating their predecessors, the Byzantines and Sassanian Imperials, whose towns and cities they had conquered. In a way this extreme worldly orientation caused the original seeds of *tasawwuf* to sprout. Hasan Al-Basri, who is supposed to have derived much of his knowledge and teachings from Imam 'Ali, was regarded as one of the earliest Sufis, without necessarily having been named as such during his life because the term 'Sufi' did not come into common use until much later. In his teachings he warned his students about the attractions, dangers and veils of the material world, reflecting what 'Ali had said: 'Asceticism is not that you should not own anything, but that nothing should own you.'

By the early eighth century an increasing number of people had chosen a way of life based on asceticism, meditative and other ritualistic practices, such as the chanting of the name of God (*Dhikr*) as a means of enhancing remembrance of Allah and maintaining self-awareness.

Mirroring the development, study and application of the legalistic and theological aspects of Islam, there was an equal rise in the practices of inner awareness, purification and self-knowledge. By the ninth century a large body of teachings from the traditions and *Sunnah* had been gathered which emphasized the importance of gaining knowledge of the self in order for higher and more subtle knowledge to become accessible.

In the writings of Al-Muhasibi (d.857) we find an early systematized form of describing the life of seekers after true knowledge. Al-Junayd (d.910), a foremost jurist of Baghdad who became the greatest Sufi master of his day, combined the inner knowledges of the self and its purification with the outer *Shari'ah*. Junayd is claimed to be the founder of many later Sufi orders that were generally accepted with Sunni norms. Shaykh 'Abdul Qadir Gilani (d.1166), also of Baghdad, was a descendant of the Prophet, a Hanbali, and the master of the great Qadiriyah Sufi order which had many branches all over the Muslim world, and whose political influence continues to our present day.

Related to the Gilani order is the Rifa'i order, established by Ahmad Al-Rifa'i (d.1181), also a descendant of the Prophet, which gave rise to the Badawi order in Egypt. Further east we have the great Shaykh 'Abdullah Al-Ansari of Herat (d.1089), whose writings have been revered by Sunni and Shi'i alike all over the Muslim world. The Bekhtashi order established by Haji Bektashi (d.1338) in eastern Anatolia emerged much later, tracing Al-Ansari as their spiritual ancestor. This order was ruthlessly put down by Kemal Ataturk.

In Iran the tradition of mysticism was much stronger than in the rest of the Muslim world mainly because it was already rooted in the past culture of the Persians. During the Marwani times many dissidents, rebels and other objectors to un-Islamic rulership found considerable sympathy in Iran.

Imam Ghazali, born and buried in north east Iran, combined mastery of the *Shari'ah* with that of *Kalam*, and during his last years his involvement with the transcendent teachings of Sufism made it acceptable to the establishment *'Ulama*. It is interesting to note that Ahmad Al-Ghazali (d.1126), the less well-known brother of Imam Ghazali, was also one of the greatest Sufis of his day, passing on much of his teachings to Abdul Qadir As-Suhrawardi (d.1167), Najmuddin Kubra (d.1221), Jalaluddin Rumi (d.1273), the founder of the Mevlevi order, and Fariduddin Attar, while many others trace the roots of their teachings back through Ahmad Al-Ghazali.

By the twelfth century *tasawwuf* was a recognized part of religious life and as such came to be taught in many *madrasahs*. Typically the term *'Irfan* was used more in Iran and the eastern territories, whereas *tasawwuf*, or knowledge of the self, was used in the western areas and North Africa. From the twelfth century onwards Sufi orders increased in number and power, politically, economically and within the religious establishment. In the western Muslim lands of North Africa they established centres called *Zawiyahs* (literally, 'corner') and *Ribats* (fortresses). From these focal centres they spread into urban and rural areas and came to exercise greater and greater influence over the new converts of North Africa and the Sahara. The Al-Murabits and the Al-Muwahids, and subsequently the Shadhilis, Qadiris and Diyanis, have all greatly affected life in the North African regions. Indeed, the Sufi orders in Africa were the mainstream of the Islamic movement and were regarded as its very heart and pinnacle of spiritual attainment. The Sanussi movement in Libya and the rise of Abdul Qadir Al-Giza'iri and others in more recent times who were independent and resisted the onslaught of Western imperialism were all based on Sufi orders.

Since the Sufis had already been flourishing from a much earlier date in the Indo-Iranian regions, their role in the spread of Islam was far greater and more established than elsewhere. Indeed, it was through Sufis and Muslim merchants rather than through organized conquest that Islam spread in the Indian sub-continent and beyond. The lands under Sassanian rule, where the Hindu and Buddhist religions had held sway before Islam, were very fertile grounds for the acceptance and flourishing of Sufism, and the first Safavid ruler was a Sufi.

A similar pattern developed in central Asia, and later we find Sufi orders forming active opposition to the hegemony of the Russian Empire in the sixteenth century. The Naqshbandi order in that region put down deep roots within the Russian Empire from the early nineteenth century, leading to several revolts and sustained opposition to the russification of Muslim lands. Imam Shamil and many other lesser known heroes were all members of Sufi orders, notably the Naqshbandis (and later on the Qadiris).

Not all the famous Sufis have exercised outer sobriety and containment. Indeed, Abu Yazid (Bayazid) Al-Bistami (d.875) expressed a great deal of ecstasy and intoxication with God. Some, like Al-Hallaj (d.922) and Suhrawardi Al-Maqtul (d.1191) were executed for what were considered blasphemous utterances.

The thirteenth century in particular produced a number of

great and still well-known Sufis, including Murcia Ibn 'Arabi (d.1240), Balkh Jalaluddin Rumi, Ibn al-Farid (d.1235) and Najmuddin Kubra (d.1221). During the fourteenth and fif-teenth centuries CE a number of great men of enlightenment such as Hyder Amuli and Sadrudin Shirazi emerged in Iran, which led to a great increase in the teachings of 'Irfan and Sufism.

During the twentieth century despite not being highly organized the Sufi movements have spread widely, and their subtle influence is present throughout Muslim lands and increasingly in the West. 'Ulama have traditionally sought outer uniformity while experiencing inner disunity, whereas the Sufis seek inner unity while tolerating outer differences.

The Sufis perfected ways of applying the teachings of Islam to the world of inner experience in a manner that was appropriate to their respective cultural climates. The sciences of the self which each group or brotherhood of Sufis developed came to be known as a Tariqah (literally, a 'way' or 'path'). Tariqah was an inner counterpoint to the Shari'ah, the combined application of which could lead to the realization of Haqiqah (Truth), that is, knowledge of God. In a tradition attributed to the Prophet, he says: 'Shari'ah is my words, Tariqah is my deeds, and Haqiqah is my inner state.' The root word of Shari'ah means path, way or waterspring; it implies outer bounds and laws. Tariqah is the passage, the movement and actual application of the teachings, injunctions and boundaries, like a car moving on the road towards its destination. Haqiqah is the Truth, being, becoming or arriving at the destined city. Recognizing the mapped road is adhering to the Shari'ah; travelling along it is Tariqah; and Haqiqah is arriving at the city of knowledge – realization.

5 · THE HISTORY OF THE MUSLIMS

In this chapter I have tried to condense as briefly as possible the history of the Muslim peoples in order to allow the meaning behind the facts and events to emerge. This is in the hope that such information will provide a basis for the reader to gain knowledge and transformation.

There are two major points to consider when looking at the history of the Muslims. The first is addressed in what the great Maghribi historian, Ibn Khaldun, identified as natural historical cycles. He describes very aptly how dynasties rise and then fall victim to their own weaknesses. He explains that the first stage in establishing a dynasty is achieved when a ruler obtains power with the support of his own people. They help to establish his rule and fight to protect his dynasty. He in turn appoints them as viziers and tax collectors, thus giving them a share of his power in important affairs.

In the second stage the ruler acts more independently from his people and claims power and glory for himself, which ferments resentment among and enmity from his people. In order to maintain his power amidst growing unrest the ruler then seeks other supporters and friends (mercenaries), not of his own kind, whom he can use against his own people if necessary.

In the third stage he falls under the power of his 'imported' supporters who, in reality, control and rule his realm. When the veil masking true control wears thin, the dynasty comes to an end and is replaced by another.

A second major point to bear in mind is the extent to which people adhere to and apply the *Din*. The development of how the life-transaction of Islam is lived parallels the natural historical evolution of rulership. Starting with fearlessness and zeal, people then settle into a domestic, inward-looking phase that then becomes diluted, dissolute and, eventually, thoroughly corrupted. At the very nadir the *Din* becomes a set of watered-down ritualistic values, far removed from the original basis of transformation.

Throughout the history of Muslims these two patterns have been recurring. Numerous cycles of rulers and the ruled, waves of growth and decline, both morally and materially, have run their course. One factor has remained fairly constant, however, which is that throughout the history of the Muslims there have always been people who have not only intellectually understood, accepted and received the message of the Qur'an and the prophetic teaching, but have also been transformed by such knowledge. Their lives have constituted living evidence of original Islam. It is this living Islam that has always been the main source and reason for Islam's spread. These transformed and enlightened men and women of knowledge – saints, Sufi masters, scholars, traders, artisans and even ordinary folk – were instrumental in the spread and rooting of Islam, for it was naturally transmitted as it was being lived.

Islam gave the early Arab Muslims a clear path to conquer the inner world of the self and save themselves from the domination of its lower tendencies. However, the conquest of the outer world and the love of and attachment to its glitter and power became so dominant that the Qur'an and the way of Muhammad were not applied sufficiently as an antidote to worldly temptation.

From the early days, Muslims became coloured and influenced by the remnants of the Byzantine and Sassanian empires, which they had taken over within a few decades after the Prophet's death. This blending enabled the Arab conquerors and their dynasties to institutionalize religion and license themselves to rule over the growing mass of

Muslims. Using old tribal loyalties, genealogy and the Arab language, it was easy to justify a certain measure of exclusivity and prestige on the part of the Sultans and Caliphs, whose personal moral qualities did not always reflect the prophetic model of conduct.

The outer strength of the Muslims, grafted as it were on to the inherited administrative machinery and style of rule of the Byzantines and Sassanians, reached its zenith during the Abbasid Empire. It was during this time that there was a great flowering of culture and civilization contained within the broadest parameters of Islam.

By the tenth and eleventh centuries CE the process of internationalizing Islam had begun, most crucially by the Turkish and Persian-speaking peoples. After Pahlavi Persian, the *lingua franca* of the far-reaching Sassanian Empire, had been modified in script from Indo-Iranian to Arabic, the monopolistic Arab neo-tribalism that had so far maintained exclusive control on the reins of power was broken. Ironically, although it was the Arabs who had brought in the Turks and Persians to serve them, these non-Arabs ended up being the new rulers, at first exercising influence from behind the throne and later ruling from it directly.

What Ibn Khaldun observed on a micro socio-historical level seems to be reflected in macro-cycles. On a macro-historical level we can see that the history of the Muslims to date falls into three phases. The extent of the true application of the Din also parallels the rise and fall of Muslim civilizations on a micro and macro scale. The first phase then starts from the Prophet and ends with the rise of the Abbasids. The second phase of international Islam begins from the end of Abbasid rule and lasts until the fourteenth century. The third phase is from then until the present day.

The first phase of empire developed almost by accident. The strong Arab tribal flavour that distinguishes this phase reflects the fact that the Arabs were sucked into the various social, political and spiritual vacuums that existed then. Almost at the end of this phase there came a crucial turning point that relaxed the Arab monopoly of Islam: the adoption of the Arabic script by a Persia which had embraced Islam. Eastern civilization (including sub-continental Asia) was at the time very much founded on the advanced Persian culture, which placed a high value on knowledge. With Islam the Persian élite had naturally learnt Arabic. By discarding the old Pahlavi script in favour of the Arabic, Islam became all the more accessible to those who lived within its ambit.

Until the end of the Abbasid Empire the spread of Islam had been an Arab phenomenon. In the second phase this was no longer the case. Exposure of Islam to the most refined and evolved culture of the time enabled the *Din* to be conveyed without being 'Arab'.

MEDINA CALIPHATE AFTER MUHAMMAD (632–661)

Immediately following the death of the Prophet there was some confusion in the Muslim community of Medina as to who should succeed him as their leader or Caliph. (Caliph is the anglicized version of *khalifah*, which is derived from the verb *khalafa*, meaning to represent or to stand for; the Qur'an describes man as having been given the authority and knowledge to be God's vicegerent on earth.) One of the tribes of Medina was about to elect a new ruler from among its leadership. Possibly more than half of Medina's inhabitants at that time comprised those who had only migrated there during the preceding two or three years. At this critical juncture old tribal rivalries, suspicions, special allegiances and the previous patterns of clannishness all surfaced.

The question of succession and authority after the Prophet is a major issue in the history of Muslims, and shapes their subsequent development and political differences. For nearly fifty years after the Prophet's death this issue (how he should be chosen and what must be done if he acts unjustly – can one disobey or depose him, for example?) was a major cause of controversy and confrontation.

During the last year of the Prophet's life three main groups amongst his Companions in Medina had become identifiable. The first group was made up of the early and faithful Companions who had migrated with him, including Abu Bakr, 'Umar, 'Ali and others. A second group were the prominent men and clans of Medina, who had enabled this migration to take place and for Islam to be established and developed in Medina. The third group were the recent converts from among the leading Meccan families, the majority of whom converted in the last two years of the Prophet's life. A few members of this last group had been the greatest enemies of the Prophet, such as Abu Sufyan and Khalid ibn al-Walid, who for many years had fought the nascent Medinan community. Many joined Islam not out of conviction and sincerity, but out of expedience for their own survival and to maintain their tribal positions of leadership. As we shall see later, it was members of this last group who, within thirty years of the Prophet's death, would take over the reins of power.

A few of the Companions who were convinced that the Prophet had already designated a successor (at Ghadir Khum) rallied around his loyal and noble cousin and son-in-law, 'Ali ibn Abi Talib, thereby planting the seeds of the Shi'i movement. The Shi'is, along with their varied associates, such as the 'Ibadis, the Zaydis and the Isma'ilis, were to play a crucial role in the development of Islamic thought and society.

However, Abu Bakr, the Prophet's elderly Companion and father of his prominent wife 'A'isha, was proclaimed the new leader. Soon after the election of Abu Bakr there was much rebellion and dissension among tribes whose political allegiance was pledged only to the leadership of the Prophet Muhammad. These wars were called the *Riddah* wars and they occupied most of Abu Bakr's caliphate (632–633).

Abu Bakr's caliphate marks the beginning of the spread of Islam beyond Arabia, and the establishment of central leadership in Medina. He and the following three Caliphs were called the *Rashidun*, or rightly guided, by the early Muslims and subsequent historians. Many of the later Caliphs and rulers acted unjustly, nor were they rightly guided, but the majority of Muslims developed the attitude of accepting their fate, as long as the ruler did not publicly go against the basic commandments of God and disrupt peace and unity among them.

'Umar's caliphate (634–644) oversees the expansion and conquest of the Fertile Crescent, northern Egypt and much of Sassanian Persia. During the time of 'Umar ibn al-Khattab the Islamic system of government and finance, as well as the military and the judiciary, began to take shape. The Muslim Arab invasion and occupation of the Syrian and Egyptian provinces of the Byzantine Empire, and the major portion of the Sassanian, within this period of time was a major event. This could only have happened with a rulership that exercised exclusive authority and the existence of a very dynamic spirit of cooperation amongst its followers, bound as they were by a strong sense of common destiny and a unifying religion.

Fighting among the Arab ranks were those who already had experience in warfare from serving the two decaying empires. The flexibility and mobility of the Arab forces using camel transport gave them a considerable advantage in these wars. This edge was amplified by the ease with which the conquered peoples accepted Arab rule, especially city dwellers, who by now did not much care who ruled over them provided they were secure and taxed reasonably. For some city folk the replacement of the Byzantines and the Iranians by the Arabs, who were tolerant of various religious groups, was a real advantage.

As the conquered areas expanded, the Arabs developed armed camps where their soldiers were garrisoned, such as Basrah and Kufah in Iraq, and Fustat in Egypt (which later became Cairo). These military camps attracted many migrants both from within Arabia and from the conquered lands, and subsequently grew into major cities. In Medina, power remained in the hands of a ruling élite, mainly comprised of the Companions of the Prophet, with a large new element from the recently converted Meccan families. The Caliph 'Umar created a system of stipends according to priority of conversion and service, thereby reinforcing the cohesion of the ruling group. Nevertheless, tribal loyalties, factional differences and claims of conversion and nobility of descent continued to beleaguer the Arabs of Medina and elsewhere. With the flow of new wealth from the north-east and the concentration of populations in Syria and Iraq, the importance of the old and established trading city of Damascus came to dominate.

Damascus had been conquered in 635, followed by other

Syrian cities. A year later in the battle of Yarmuk near the Jordan River the Byzantine Emperor's brother was killed, and the rest of Syria opened up to the Muslims. In 637 the Sassanian army led by Rustam was crushed at Qadisiyyah near Hirah, and their capital at Ctesiphon was taken. By 641 no Sassanian power remained west of the Zagros mountains. Jerusalem and Khuzistan were taken in 638, Egypt was invaded and Fustat established on the site of a Roman castle called Babylon. Alexandria was taken in 642 and Tripolitania raided. A year later the Makran coast (now in Pakistan) was laid open.

'Umar left Medina for the first time to receive the keys of Jerusalem. With consideration for the feelings of the Christian population, when it was time for his prayers he left the church of the Holy Cross in order to pray outside, so as not to set a precedent for other Muslims to take over the churches from the Christians. During his absence from Medina 'Ali Ibn Abi Talib acted as his deputy.

It was during 'Umar's time that the year of migration (*Hijrah*) was adopted as the starting point of the Muslim calendar. 'Umar was fifty-two years old when he was assassinated by a Persian craftsman who had been brought to Medina to embellish the formerly humble mud dwellings of the inhabitants. 'Umar's assassination left a group of Medina elders to choose his successor. They chose the weakest among them, a pious early convert and son-in-law of the Prophet, 'Uthman ibn 'Affan.

'Uthman belonged to a branch of the Quraysh tribe, many of whose members were late converts and former enemies of the Prophet. He appointed numerous members of his clan to be provisional governors. This aroused resentment and increasing agitation among both the older Companions in Medina and the new generation of Muslims, including the Prophet's wife 'A'isha, and considerable discontent emanated from the cantonments of Kufah and Fustat. The domination of the new clan from Mecca was resented to such an extent that as unrest grew in Medina, supported by soldiers from Egypt, 'Uthman was murdered in 656.

It was during 'Uthman's caliphate (644–656) that the conquest of Iran and Egypt was completed and consolidated, bringing new luxuries to the wealthy families of Medina, and heralding a phase of worldly competition and acquisitiveness.

Under 'Uthman, the Qur'an was written according to the original Qurayshi dialect (it had originally been revealed in seven *ahruf* or local dialects) and distributed to the provinces to arrest any future differences and misunderstandings. On the administrative side 'Uthman allowed the rulers of the provinces to exercise considerable power at their own discretion.

As Muslim sea-power grew, Cyprus was taken in 649. Persepolis, the chief city of Fars and the centre of the Zoroastrian religion, was also taken, and Yazdagird, the last Sassanian ruler, was assassinated in Khurasan in 651. Between 652 and 654 Sicily, Rhodes and other Mediterranean ports came under Muslim rule, and in the year 655 the Muslims defeated the Byzantine forces commanded by the Emperor on the south-west Anatolian coast.

'Uthman's death marks the first period of civil war and bloodshed in the Muslim community, resulting in the popular election of 'Ali Ibn Abi Talib as the fourth Caliph. 'Ali soon abandoned the city of Medina, which had become turbulent since 'Uthman's murder, and established himself in Kufah. 'Uthman's kin used 'Ali's failure to seek out and punish those responsible for 'Uthman's murder to oppose the new Caliph. There were also other power groups whose interest ran against the election of such an ascetic, courageous and uncompromising leader.

In demanding punishment for the murderers of 'Uthman, the Prophet's wife 'A'isha, along with two of his associates, accused 'Ali of laxity in applying justice. Mutiny and dissidence erupted in the camp sites of the Fertile Crescent, culminating in the Battle of the Camel near the garrison city of Basrah. 'A'isha, who had led the opposition to 'Ali on her camel, was handled firmly but graciously and returned to Medina, whereby 'Ali was declared Caliph in Kufah and recognized by most of the provinces. The notable exception was Mu'awiyah (a cousin of 'Uthman), the governor of Syria, who by now had vowed to avenge 'Uthman's death.

Mu'awiyah had already been governor in Syria for some twenty years. As the son of Abu Sufyan, he had inherited the leadership of the Umayyad clan which had a well-trained army considered to be the largest and most organized in Muslim lands at that time. The indigenous Syrian Arabs regarded Mu'awiyah as a legitimate successor to their old Ghassani princely house, for his wife was an aristocrat of the south Arabian tribe of Kalb, the most powerful in Syria.

In order to overcome the mutiny in Syria, 'Ali marched towards the upper Euphrates to a confrontation at Siffin in 657. After the battle it was decided to settle the matter through delegates chosen by both sides. A large group of 'Ali's supporters (who later became known as the *Kharijis*, literally, the 'seceders') abandoned him, accusing him of leniency and compromise on the issue of caliphate. Although most of these rebels were later defeated by 'Ali, their movement spread elsewhere and considerably influenced the development of Muslim politics and thought (particularly with regard to sin and authority). Though Mu'awiyah's forces suffered much during the fighting at Siffin, the truce and arbitration that had been agreed upon backfired and consequently compromised 'Ali, reducing his authority. In 661, during the dawn prayers at the mosque in Kufah, 'Ali was martyred by a *Khariji*.

'Ali's followers, the Shi'i, transferred their allegiance to his appointed successor, his son Hasan, who also accepted a truce with Mu'awiyah in order to avoid bloodshed, for he realized that his people would be cheated by Mu'awiyah. After securing Hasan's capitulation, Mu'awiyah brazenly declared himself the Caliph in Damascus, thereby establishing the first hereditary Muslim dynastic rule.

THE DAMASCUS CALIPHATE: Ummayyad Clan Rule – the Mu'awiyah Clan (661–692) and the Marwani Clan (692–750)

The early battles and wars fought during the first few decades after the *Hijrah* – such as Badr, Uhud and many others – were clearly battles by Islam against *kufr*. Very few battles were corrective, that is, fought within the Muslim communities, such as those undertaken by Abu Bakr and 'Ali. The battles of Qadisiyyah, Yarmuk and those in North Africa and Andalus were all fought in the way of Islamic expansion. However, with the establishment of dynastic rule in Damascus, internal power struggles within the ruling élite were to be a continuous cause of instability and strife.

Arab rule through the caliphate based in Damascus falls into two periods, the first ruled by Mu'awiyah I (661–680) and his short-lived descendants, and the second by the Marwanis, beginning in 692 under 'Abdul Malik.

Mu'awiyah managed to stamp out revolts and dissidence, establishing centralized administration with strong loyalty and obedience to him. From his time onwards rulership and government became hereditary and dynastic. Many pious Muslims regard this era as that of betrayal and subversion of the true original prophetic model.

In the name of Islam an empire was created, taking as its capital the ancient Byzantine city of Damascus and adopting the administrative, political and military machinery of the defunct Byzantine government. From this point on most Muslim rulers and their governments grew more concerned with self-preservation, power, accumulating wealth and controlling their people. The prophetic way of piety and submission to Allah's decree, establishing justice and Islam, came to be upheld only at face value.

From being tribal chieftains the new Caliphs imitated the traditional lifestyle of the rulers of Byzantium and later that of the Sassanian dynasties. Governing such a great empire undoubtedly resulted in many moral compromises and the forging of new allegiances, thus diluting and misinterpreting original Islam. A new ruling group of Arab chieftains and army commanders formed the governing élite, thereby reducing the importance and influence of the old noble families in Medina and Mecca.

Mu'awiyah managed to manipulate the Muslims very effectively by keeping alive a collective religious spirit, maintaining morale and fervour among them, and by using less zealous and more flexible interpreters of Islam to uphold his court and personal despotism. He appointed Ziyad ibn Abih (a bastard and therefore technically ineligible to hold office) to govern the former Sassanian areas, and publicly declared that Ziyad was the legitimate son of his father (hence his name which means 'son of his father'). Most significantly, during his lifetime he ensured that the Muslims recognize his unworthy son Yazid as his successor, despite having promised to Hasan that upon his death the caliphate would revert to Hasan.

Yazid ruled for four turbulent years (680–683), which were preoccupied with internal battles and wars. The old Muslim families of Medina refused to recognize him because of his corrupt and decadent behaviour. His bouts of violent drunkenness and moral bankruptcy were well known.

When the old Muslim families of Medina rose up in revolt, the grandson of the Prophet, Husayn (the son of 'Ali and Fatima, Muhammad's daughter) was invited by the Kufan people to assume the leadership (imamate) of the community. In 680 Husayn and some seventy members of his family and companions set out towards Kufah, but before they arrived the Syrian-appointed governor managed to gain control over the rebellious Kufans. Husayn and his household were then isolated and massacred in the desert of Karbala, near Kufah. His martyrdom and burial in that place sowed the seeds of numerous future revivals and uprisings. His shrine at Karbala and that of 'Ali at Kufah (now called Najaf) were among the earliest to be frequented by visitors from all over the Muslim world.

In the meantime, 'Abdullah ibn Az-Zubayr, the son of the great Companion of the Prophet (who had opposed 'Ali after the death of 'Uthman), rose in Medina. In Syria the tribe of Kalb (associated with Mu'awiyah) fought against him, while he was supported by another major tribe, the Qays.

Marwan ibn al-Hakam, a cousin of Mu'awiyah's, who had been very close to 'Uthman as his chief advisor (considered by some to have been in effect the real ruler), emerged as the most influential figure during the last year of Yazid's reign. This was despite the fact that he was the only person whom the Prophet had ever exiled. While Abu Bakr as first Caliph had been pressurized to allow him to return, 'Umar had banished him further and it was only during 'Uthman's time (for he was a kinsman) that the gates for his re-entry were thrown open.

In Iran and Arabia, groups of Kharijis had set up separate regimes upholding their puritanical and zealous attitude, making no distinction between Arab and non-Arab, provided that the leader was just, egalitarian and free of moral error.

Yazid died in 683 and was survived by a young son Mu'awiyah II who also soon died, leaving the power in Marwan's hands. The Marwani forces attacked Medina forthwith, and after much destruction conquered the city, leaving it devastated as they turned to besiege Mecca. Ibn Az-Zubayr prevailed, however, for a considerable length of time until 692, when he was defeated and killed at Mecca.

Marwan I was succeeded by his son 'Abdul Malik who within a few years managed to establish the confidence of the Arabs in their future destiny as the people 'selected by God' to spread His message. During his rulership (685–705) the Arabic language was introduced for the first time in government administration. New coins were struck, and monumental buildings were constructed for the rulers and the wealthy. Palaces as well as mosques sprang up everywhere heralding the establishment of the new order. The Marwani Umayyad Dynasty continued from 692 to 750 when the Abbasids, another branch of the tribe of Quraysh, took over.

By unequivocally using force and tribal allegiance, and playing on religious sentiment, 'Abdul Malik established an empire. His lieutenant, al-Hajjaj bin Yusuf, brought Mecca and its people into total subservience as he damaged the Ka'bah and ruled over the Sassanian dominions with ruthless cunning and determination. The Iraqi Muslims were all terrorized into submission and forced to pay allegiance to Hajjaj at the new provincial town, Wasit, which he built midway between Basrah and Kufah.

In 705 'Abdul Malik was smoothly succeeded by his son, al-Walid, during whose reign both Spain and Sind were conquered. Al-Walid's succession heralds an uninterrupted half-century of the continuation and consolidation of Marwani rule in Damascus, later resumed in Muslim Spain.

A significant event in the expansion of Islam to take place during al-Walid's reign was the submission of the Berbers following an intensive Muslim onslaught from Tunis. Although conversion to Islam was not always the main objective of the Arab rulers, they had come to take it for granted that Islam was given to the Arabs in order for them to rule, rather than as a superior way of life for all mankind. However, Berber tribalism was similar to that of the Arabs, as they lived nomadically on the margins of urban civilization in the mountainous regions of the Maghreb.

The Berbers were converted to Islam *en masse*. Once they had accepted the superiority of the Arabs, they joined them, taking pride in their close association. The subsequent conquests of the Spanish peninsula would have been impossible without the Berber fighters and settlers.

The conquest of Sind by both land and sea was easy as many of the Buddhist peoples preferred the Muslims to the Hindu ruling classes, for the Muslims brought greater human tolerance, justice and acceptance of other religions which were guaranteed protection under Islamic law.

The strength of the Marwani style of rule was based on Arab tribalistic networks and connections. Arab clans and tribes had installed themselves all over this enormous empire which stretched from Spain to China, establishing themselves as the new territorial landowners.

Factional fighting amongst the Arab tribal blocs sustained a continuous power struggle among the Muslims. Many of the old tribal attitudes and traditions that were deeply rooted in the primitive ways of pre-Islam spread over into these new lands. In many of these newly conquered regions being an Arab was considered more important than being a Muslim. For a Muslim to participate in the political arena he often had to affiliate himself as a client (*mawla*; plural: *mawali*) of an Arab clan. As the old Bedouin values took root with their hosts, they often came to be accepted as Islamic in the new territories. Preserved and reinforced by the Arabic language, tribal loyalty and dependence, many aspects of pagan Arabian ways were thus adapted to new urban conditions, in spite of what the Qur'an revealed: 'Certainly the nomadic Arabs are intense in hypocrisy and denial of truth' (9:97).

One notable exception to the tribally focused Arabian style of rule was that of 'Umar Ibn 'Abdul 'Aziz, generally known as 'Umar II (717–720). He succeeded Walid I mainly as a result of the feuds and infighting among the Arab solidery. Walid had initially been succeeded by Sulayman (715–717), during whose time the warfare between the Qays and Kalb reached its zenith. It was also during his time that the conquerors of Andalus, Tariq ibn Ziyad and the Governor

Musa ibn Nusayr, returned to be humiliated and to die in dejected obscurity.

'Umar's personal piety and sincere Islamic conviction and behaviour became a proud example that Muslims still remember. He reconciled many of the Shi'is as well as the Kharijis, restored the dignity of the Prophet's family, and rectified much of the subversion and derailment of Islam that had already taken place. However, he was succeeded by Yazid II (720–724) who, like his brother Sulayman, was given to women and song. Both brothers were despised by pious Muslims, so notorious were they for their lives of frivolous pleasures and cruelty.

Hisham (724–743) improved the bureaucratic organization and centralized control of the caliphate by using talented non-Muslims as well as Muslims for administration and rule. His became the subsequent model for other absolute rulers to imitate, and some of his many new administrative tools were taken to Spain. Regular confiscation, arbitrary arrest, torture and spying were commonly used as official weapons against anyone who incurred the displeasure of the ruler. Harsh and un-Islamic measures were often used against officials and governors in his employ, many of whom were corrupt and given to embezzlement.

Al-Walid II (743–744), Hisham's successor, was notorious for his immorality and lack of political acumen. The well-entrenched Kalb tribesmen agitated against him and he was killed and replaced by Yazid III.

Through Marwani rule, what had been a collection of occupied territories was transformed into a unified Empire ruled centrally from Damascus. With the growth of the Marwani Empire, factional fighting increased as tribal differences became accentuated by rival claims to noble descent. A long-standing confrontation between the Qays and Kalb tribes, of northern and southern origin respectively, often erupted. In Muslim Spain, tribal affiliations and loyalties were often called on whenever it suited the rulers.

Resentment began to grow among the new converts to Islam, especially among those of non-Arab origin, such as the Persians. Fiscal discrimination and the obvious privileges given to those of Arab origin were among the causes of the subsequent revolt against Umayyad rule. As the Shi'is,

Kharijis and many other smaller groups opposed Marwani rule, they gained considerable momentum in the eastern provinces, particularly in Khurasan, where they rose so rapidly that they brought about the sudden collapse of the Marwanis, whereupon numerous groups of pious Muslims, who hoped to restore Islamic values and the prophetic model, joined in the rising tide of opposition. This revolution culminated in establishing the Abbasi clan, another branch of the tribe of Quraysh, as the new rulers of the Muslim Empire.

ABBASID EMPIRE AND HIGH CULTURE (750–945)

Since the martyrdom of Imam Husayn in 680 many discontented Muslim groups had been in regular revolt against the caliphate. In Khurasan the Arab settlers had been assimilated into Iranian society and had welcomed the emissary from Kufah, Abu Muslim, who had been sent to rally them by the descendants of the Prophet's uncle, 'Abbas. Abu Muslim managed to assemble a sizeable army incorporating most of the dissident elements, Arab and otherwise, under the Prophet's black banner. It was this army that moved westward from Khurasan to defeat the Umayyads in a series of battles between the years 749 and 750.

Marwan II was pursued to Egypt and killed there. To the disappointment of the Shi'is, the new leader, Abu'l-'Abbas, was proclaimed Caliph in Kufah. Between 749 and 754 he ruled with an iron fist, exercising brutal power. His first act was to kill Abu Muslim and many of the other leaders who had helped bring him to power. He himself was killed by his brother, the ruthless al-Mansur.

One of the principal achievements of al-Mansur (754–775) was to build a new capital, Baghdad, not far from Ctesiphon. Baghdad's location was of strategic importance, being located in fertile country beside the river Tigris, and close to the river Euphrates on the main route leading to Iran and beyond.

Al-Mansur combined all the pomp and grandeur of the Byzantine Emperors with that of the Sassanian. His capital was built expressly to highlight the splendour and power, as well as the exalted, majestic 'distance' of the ruler. Muslim emperorship surpassed that of all their predecessors of the vanquished empires by adding to their office the religious stamp of being God's vicegerents on earth. Under al-Mansur ('the victorious' – his naming signifies a new era in grandiose titling), the position of ruler was raised from being a simple commander among equal believers to a remote and magnificent figure in a world of awesome luxury, separate from the populace. The court at Baghdad might have adorned itself with Islamic garb and ritual, but it was modelled on that of the Sassanian Empire. Access to the Abbasid Caliph could only be had through a most cumbersome chain of officials in accordance with highly stylized protocol.

In reality, the Abbasid rulers were only extending and completing the imperial edifice developed by 'Abdul Malik and Hisham. The symbol of the Caliph's power was the executioner, who always stood beside him, ready with the sword and leathern mat.

Whereas the ultimate power of the Caliph had previously rested upon the garrison townships, the building of Baghdad epitomized the new concentration of absolute power. The entire city was built in order to service the court and administrative complex, at the centre of which was the Caliph's palace. This urban pattern was later emulated by many Muslim potentates from Andalusia to the Asian sub-continent.

The exalted name of al-Mahdi (meaning 'the rightly guided' – it was only later that this name came to be used by the Shi'ah for the expected restorer and saviour of Islam) was given to al-Mansur's son, who ruled from 775–785. Al-Mahdi was pious and sought to reconcile the '*Ulama* of his day. By the time of his death the monarchy had gained a certain measure of institutional religious support.

After the brief reign of al-Mahdi's eldest son, al-Hadi, he was succeeded by his younger son, Harun al-Rashid (Aaron the Wise, 786–808). The Empire at this time was at the zenith of its splendour, culture and centralized power. Administration was delegated to a vizier, who acted as head of government with many secretaries and bureaus called *Diwans* (the French word *douane*, meaning 'customs', derives from this word) working under him. Revenue came from land tax as well as from the poll tax on non-Muslims, and dues were also levied on imported and exported goods.

The period of classical, imperial Abbasid rule was accompanied by considerable development and recording of the institution of religion based on the Qur'an and the prophetic traditions and their interpretations. The teachings of Imam Ja'far as-Sadiq (d. 765) and the emergence of the Iraqi school of *fiqh* through Abu Hanifah (d.767) was to be followed by the work of Malik ibn Anas (d.795), the Imam of Medina. In parallel, we notice the emergence of Sufis reviving the original spirit of Islam.

During the time of al-Rashid most of the army in Baghdad was comprised of newly recruited soldiers from the Turkic-speaking tribes of central Asia. The Turks were essentially mercenaries in the Caliph's pay. Their recruitment later formed a major turning point in the power-base of Muslim rule, as the imported protectors of the Arab masters eventually became the rulers themselves.

Al-Rashid was publicly known to be a wine-drinker. The celebrated court poet, Abu Nuwas (d.803), much favoured by him, was associated with wine and gaiety of song. The most self-respecting 'Ulama, therefore, avoided being identified with al-Rashid, although both he and his court honoured the scholars of Shari'ah.

After al-Rashid's death civil war erupted between his two sons, al-Amin and al-Ma'mun. Though al-Rashid had already divided his Empire between them, giving the western portion to the former and the eastern portion to the latter, the Empire was later reunited under al-Ma'mum after his troops defeated those of al-Amin at Baghdad.

Al-Ma'mun (813–833) made serious attempts to win over other Muslim factions, especially the Shi'ah, by drawing close to and proclaiming as his successor the eighth Shi'i Imam, 'Ali al-Rida (now buried in Mashhad, Iran). The Imam found himself in a very difficult position, and in order to safeguard the interests of his followers he reluctantly allowed this proclamation to take place.

Inclining to the Mu'tazilite application of logic and reasoning, al-Ma'mun endowed a great research library called Bayt al-Hikmah (the House of Wisdom), filling it with manuscripts from Constantinople and elsewhere. Natural sciences, medicine, astronomy and mathematics, as well as philosophy, were promoted greatly in translation and documentation.

After al-Ma'mun, the Caliph al-Mu'tasim moved his capital from Baghdad to a newly built city called Sammarra, north of Baghdad, on the river Tigris. The Turkish mercenaries had by now become the mainstay of the caliphate's power, mostly being limited to the cities and the surrounding agricultural areas. From around the ninth century onwards governors of far-flung provinces were given greater autonomy and power to collect taxes and employ local forces in maintaining law and order. Wherever possible, central control was maintained through a system of intelligence.

The caliphate of al-Wathiq (842–847) represents the last phase of Abbasid rule over a centrally dominated Empire. His successor, al-Mutawakkil (847–861), gave much support to the Hadith-minded 'Ulama, and developed ingenious ways of persecuting the Shi'is and other dissidents, but ended up being the first Caliph to be murdered by his Turkish soldiers. After his death and until 949 the Abbasid centralized power was steadily eroded. Province after province became almost independent until the caliphate lost fiscal and political control. In the meantime, economic, cultural and social life had flourished in different parts of the Muslim world, with colourful variations resulting from the integration of old and new ways, cross-fertilized by newcomers to Islam.

Al-Muntasir (861–862), al-Musta'in (862–866) and al-Mu'tazz (866–869) were virtual puppets in the hands of their Turkish soldiers, although the Caliph al-Mu'tamid (879–892) was enabled by his brother, al-Muwafaq, to re-establish more effective authority between Syria and Khurasan.

Although the Abbasid caliphate remained intact for three more centuries, effective power was in the hands of other dynasties, supported by military groups, who continued to recognize the caliphate in name and form only. As the Arabs' hold on the caliphate weakened, numerous dynasties (Arab and otherwise) sprang up under its broad canopy, including the Samanids in Khurasan (819–1005), the Zaydi Shi'i state on the Caspian (864–928), and Ibn al-Tulun and his son in Cairo (868–906). The Aghlabids ruled in Tunisia (800–909) and conquered Sicily, which they held until the late eleventh century. The Buyids, a family of military leaders, took over effective power in Baghdad in 945, adopting the extravagant Iranian title of King of Kings (Shahinshah) for their monarch. In Mosul, and later in Aleppo, the Hamdanis, who supported the Shi'is, established autonomous rule between 905 and 979.

Replacing the Aghlabids, the Isma'ili Fatimid caliphate was established in the Maghreb between 909–972. The Fatimids occupied Egypt in 969, and from there extended their power over western Arabia and Syria. Their rulers assumed the tiles of both Imam and Caliph, giving open expression to rulership that combined the spiritual with the temporal. Their government imitated the caliphate in Baghdad in the use of elaborate ceremonial protocol while their army, drawn mostly from outside Egypt, was composed of Berbers, Turks and Sudanese, among others.

In Spain a new formal challenge to the Abbasid caliphate was made when 'Abdur Rahman III assumed the title of Caliph (912–961). Towards the end of the eighth century, Idris, a great-grandson of 'Ali Ibn Abi Talib, escaped persecution in Medina, reached Morocco where he won the support of the newly converted Berbers, and thereby established a dynasty which was to greatly influence the history of North Africa. His son, Mulay Idris, built the city of Fez, where he lies buried. All subsequent rulers of Morocco have justified their claims to rulership partly by their descent from the Prophet, and almost exclusively through Mulay Idris and Imam Hasan.

The importation of Turkish soldiery and the lack of a sufficiently established civil administration independent of the ruler's person gradually eroded and diluted Abbasid power which allowed provincial governors and local rulers to become, in effect, autonomous. However, the ultimate break-up of the Abbasid caliphate actually revitalized the growth and development of culture among Muslims. It had long suited the purpose of numerous local rulers to acknowledge the symbolic unifying banner of the Abbasids beyond the time when its power had begun to pall. With their demise, the remote cloud of the unifying caliphate was lifted. The Mongols simply walked over the central territories and actualized the powerlessness of Abbasid central rule which had existed for so long.

MUSLIM SPAIN

The history of the Muslims in Spain represents a special and significant period that reflects similarities as well as differences with the spread of Islam elsewhere. The culture of Muslim Andalusia was born of the interaction between Arabs, Berbers and Europeans, all influenced or inspired by Islam. For students of Islamic culture and civilization, and the relationship between distinct social, racial, political and religious groups, Andalusia presents a very rich world for study, for it was a microcosm of the entire Muslim world.

The Arab name given to Muslim Spain – Jazirat al-Andalus – is a variation of 'Vandals' who, with the Visigoths, had ruled in Iberia under a weakened Roman Empire. The term 'Vandals' had been used by the Christians of the late Roman Empire to denigrate these much feared warriors (hence 'vandalism').

EARLY CONQUEST (711–756)

The Arabs and Berbers first landed in Spain in 710, when Tariq ibn Ziyad (a Berber) invaded with an expeditionary force. Arab Muslims had by that time already established a strong presence in Tunis, having founded the garrison town of Qayrawan south of Carthage, in 667. The following year (711) Tariq crossed with a force of Berbers estimated at 9,000 and defeated Roderick at Wadi Luqa. He was soon joined by the capable and ambitious North African Governor of the Marwani rule, Musa ibn Nusayr, and the Arabs and Berbers of the first settlement were soon joined by a new wave of Arabs from Syria.

After a period during which the Muslim Arabs established their rule in numerous fiefdoms, one of the grandsons of the Caliph Hisham, 'Abdur Rahman I (from Damascus) managed to defuse the power struggle between the various commanders and governors and to consolidate his power over them, thereby effectively becoming the first ruler of Andalusia (756–788). His escape from Damascus, exile to Morocco and subsequent rule over Andalus make fascinating reading. It was he who initiated the construction of the Great Mosque of Cordova, importing trees, rugs, and many other furnishings, as well as skilled artisans, from the East.

The speed and extent of the Muslim takeover of the Iberian peninsula was overwhelming by any standard. Within a decade, a few thousand warriors controlled vast territories. It seemed the sky was the limit, though the sea and mountains to the north formed natural boundaries. Nonetheless, in spite of the rich rewards of al-Andalus, the Muslims crossed the Pyrenees with very little resistance until their diluted and exhausted force was stopped at Poitiers.

European historians make much of the battle at Poitiers, where Charles Martel defeated the Arab Muslim forces led by 'Abdur Rahman al-Ghafiqi in 732. Arab historians, however, either ignore it completely, or treat it as a raid of no historical significance.

GROWTH AND DECAY

The new Umayyad dynasty founded by 'Abdur Rahman I was to last for three hundred years. However, Muslim rule in the peninsula continued until 1492, though on a diminished scale, when the last kingdom in Granada was conquered by the Christian forces of Fernando and Isabella.

'Abdur Rahman's rule was based upon an alliance between Arab tribes and Berbers to whom he was affiliated through his mother. He was succeeded by Hisham I, who in turn was succeeded by al-Hakim and then by 'Abdur Rahman II (822–852), during which time there was great cultural, artistic and commercial florescence. The Mosque of Cordova was enlarged, and the school of Maliki jurisprudence was established. Scholars and 'Ulama would bring in updated religious scholarship and greater definition to theological discipline and learning. Andalusian poetry and music flourished to such an extent that artists from all the Muslim lands were drawn there, including Ziryab, a singer from Baghdad, who gained immense popularity and cultural influence among the political élite.

As the Arab Muslims settled in Andalusia, luxury goods and fine art became important to their way of life. Many of the merchants on the long trade routes were Jews, who organized the export of Spanish silk, metalwork, olive oil and other produce across the North African coast through Tunis and further east. A large number of Berbers cultivated the land on the higher ground and nearer to the coast that looked across to their former homeland. Their skills in terrace cultivation opened up much new land for agriculture. Many of the terraces in present-day Andalusia, and indeed throughout Spain, were the work of these Berbers. It was during this time that hydrological technology (the waterwheel and so on) was imported from Syria, and the system of canals (*qanat*) from Iran. Other agrarian technologies and techniques (such as crop rotation) were also introduced at this time.

From the year 852 to 912 there was a succession of rulers that reflected a period of both internal and external instability. Decentralized rule allowed for weakened law and order. The new generations of Muslims born of Arab stock and indigenous mothers were called *Muwallad* ('born one'). Christians living among Muslims were called *Mozarab* ('arabized'), while Muslims living under Christian rule were known as *Mudejar* (domesticated and therefore not to be feared). Old tribal, ethnic and clannish rivalries between the Arabs, Berbers and Muwallads would sometimes flare up into confrontations, and by the tenth century fear of Christian attacks from the north had begun to be realized.

The flowering of Andalusian civilization reached its peak during the reign of 'Abdur Rahman III (912–961). Upon his succession he had to contend with the legacy of numerous upheavals incited by pretenders to the throne within the ruling clan. Once he had consolidated his power, a unified Andalusia was able to counteract external threats. The accompanying internal prosperity brought out the ultimate in self-acclaim when he declared himself Caliph in 921. This caliphate was to compete with that of the Fatimids and the weakened Abbasids until 1031, when it was abolished.

Among the legacies of 'Abdur Rahman's reign is the lavish palace city of al-Zahra, for which huge quantities of luxurious furnishings were imported from the East. He also introduced the Slavs as mercenaries to counteract internal factional fighting between the Arabs and Berbers. The Slavs – called *saqalibah*, meaning 'from Siqilya' (Sicily) – later gained great power in Andalusia.

'Abdur Rahman was succeeded by al-Hakam II (961–976) who encouraged and was personally interested in theology, jurisprudence and other religious matters. He wrote several books, founded libraries and patronized scholarship. He was followed by a period of political weakening and subsequent disintegration, lawlessness and bloodshed. Rulers made numerous alliances and broke them, both within the tribal systems as well as with the Christian kingdoms to the north.

The years 1031–1090 are marked by the emergence of numerous emirates and kingdoms centred around power groups led by the so-called 'Faction' Kings. Of up to nine clearly defined kingdoms, one was called Denia, where the Emir Mujahid built up a sizeable naval fleet and temporarily ruled Sardinia. His Christian wife and son, 'Ali, were taken prisoner by the German Emperor and kept captive for many years. Although 'Ali grew up in the court of the Holy Roman Emperor, he later returned to Andalusia to become a future king. With the freshness of one who has discovered the true meaning of his spiritual patrimony, 'Ali established justice and harmony within his state and with his neighbours, but ended up being taken captive to Saragosa in 1076 by his brother-in-law.

The period of the Faction Kings was a time of worldly competition, anarchy, confusion and battle. From 1057 onwards, the Christian kingdoms of the north exacted tributes from most of these kings until, in 1085, Toledo fell to Alfonso IV, while Valencia was taken by the famous El Cid (whose name was derived from the Arabic honorific *sidi*, meaning 'my master' or 'lord').

The eleventh century marks the beginning of the end of Muslim rule in Spain. With the first Crusade in 1098, outside influences were brought into Andalusia. When Muslim rule in Sicily ended in 1091, Arab supremacy in the Mediterranean was brought to an end.

THE ALMORAVIDS, OR AL-MURABITS

Around the middle of the eleventh century there was much social, religious and political activity in North Africa, culminating in the building of the city of Marrakesh in 1062. In 1075 the entire Maghreb came under the control of the al-Murabits, who ruled from 1076 to 1147. Their strength lay in the same qualities as those of their successors: a combination of instigating religious reform and revival, backed by the potent force of the Berbers.

Al-Andalus became a province of the al-Murabits from 1090 to 1145. After being invited to help resolve the bickering between the Muslim kings of the Iberian Peninsula, Ibn Tashfin came to the peninsula in 1090 and systematically liquidated the quarrelsome Andalusian rulers. Ironically, the King (al-Mu'tamid), who had first invited him to help, later begged for assistance against him and received it from the Christian King Alfonso. The al-Murabits initially led a pious and austere spiritual life. They ended up controlling a vast empire that included most of Spain.

Under the al-Murabits, religious scholarship gained more prestige. A rigorous application of the law was established at the expense of other creative, philosophical or speculative development. Al-Ghazali's books were burnt, and attempts to bring reasoning into religious scholarship were banned. The al-Murabit dynasty, however, soon succumbed to the degeneration of luxurious excess, enabling the Almohads (al-Muwahhidun, the unitarians), who were rising under similar circumstances in the Maghreb, to become the new masters of Andalusia, as well as of North Africa.

THE ALMOHADS, OR AL-MUWAHIDDUN

The Almohads were also of Berber origin and ruled from 1121 to 1296. They were founded by Muhammad ibn Tumart from the region of Sus, who was much influenced by Al-Ghazali's teachings, combining orthodoxy with some Mu'tazilite elements. His successor took Marrakesh in 1130, and by 1163 the Almohads had marched into Andalus with an army estimated at 200,000 men.

By the early thirteenth century the Andalusian political map was divided into three Christian spheres of influence: Castille, Aragon and Portugal. As the Christian settlements and military outposts became increasingly established and the Christians moved on to the offensive, the Almohads faced the impossible task of trying to contain this onslaught from their seat of rule in Marrakesh after the reign of the last great Almohad, Ya'qub, (1184–1199).

While Muslim rule in al-Andalus gradually disintegrated, the Almohad dynasty lingered on in Africa until 1269, when they were replaced in Tunisia by the Hafsids and in Morocco by the Marinids.

GRANADA

The Nasrid dynasty (1231–1492) began in Granada with Muhammad Bin Yusuf bin Ahmed bin Nasir ibn al-Ahmar, who helped Fernando II of Castille to capture Cordova in 1236. He ruled over Malaga, Almiria and Granada, while paying tribute to the Christians. He further assisted Fernando in seizing Seville in 1248, which discredited him in the eyes of the Muslim population. By 1264, however, he was so overpowered by the Christians that he desperately sought help from the Marinids (who eventually assisted his son) to repulse the attacking Christians.

The construction of the Al-Hambra palace which he had initiated was continued by his son Muhammad II (1273–1301). Whilst the rural areas developed in all social and economic aspects, the standard of living in the city of Granada was amongst the highest in the world at that time.

After Muhammad, internecine feuds, assassinations, and bloodshed, as well as intrigues involving the ladies of the palace, all became the norm. The reign of Yusuf III (1407–1413) was the last period of relative stability as he managed to stave off the attacking Christians, who had by now surrounded his kingdom. After him the kingdom remained in a perpetual state of unrest. The vulnerable Granadines appealed to Egypt and the Ottomans for help but to no avail.

The last tragic episodes before the fall of Granada are centred around Boabdil, whose full name was Abu 'Abdullah

Muhammad bin 'Ali. He was to succeed his father in 1482, but was taken prisoner in an expedition against the Castillians. He eventually took office in 1487, after being released upon payment of a ransom to Fernando V of Aragon.

After Aragon and Castille were united, Fernando V was constantly pressured by the clergy to capture Granada. Fernando marched into Granada with a large army, demanding that Boabdil surrender. The leaders of the community and the jurists insisted that he refuse. Fernando withdrew, only to return in 1491, besieging Granada for over seven months. Boabdil accepted surrender upon apparently favourable terms, guaranteeing Muslims their rights of religion, culture and language. Granada was entered and occupied on 2nd January 1492.

The terms of surrender were soon brushed aside and Boabdil was forced to leave the country and give up his estate and other privileges agreed upon under the terms of surrender. He left for Fez and was soon followed by many Granadines. From 1499 onwards Fernando and his Queen Isabella subjected the Muslim population of Granada to extreme hardship. They demanded complete effacement of their culture, ruthlessly putting down any sign of dissension. This suppression continued until 1639–41, when the last remaining Muslims were expelled.

Andalusian society was made up of a mixture of Muslims, Jews and Christians. There were Arabs, Berbers, indigenous Spaniards, new converts and soldiers of fortune from western and eastern Europe. These diverse peoples were held together by the Umayyad rule from Cordova, backed by an Andalusian élite claiming Arab descent from the early settlers. The prestige and power of the ruling élite were expressed in magnificent architecture, poetry and other cultured practices. The distinctive style of mosque construction, especially that of Cordova with its multiple aisles and marble pillars surmounted by horseshoe arches, was the fruit of the combined genius of the disciplined Germanic Gothic mind and the Muslim spirit and influence, brought in part from the East and adapted for space and ease of movement for the worshippers. Later the Almoravids and Almohads built a number of great mosques in Andalus, Morocco, Algeria and Tunisia. The Qarawiyyin mosque in Fez, built by the Almoravids, was much imitated all over Morocco. The most impressive monument in al-Andalus is without doubt the Al-Hambra palace in Granada, built as a royal city, at the heart of which was the palace, set high above and separate from the main city which lay below.

Religious temperament was generally austere, based on Maliki law. However, Muslim Spain did produce many great philosophers, thinkers and Sufi masters, such as Averroes, Ibn Bajjah, Ibn 'Arabi and Ibn Tufayl.

The two languages spoken by most of the Muslims, Christians and Jews were Andalusian Arabic and a Romance dialect which later developed into Spanish. However, for the written word, classical Arabic was used by the Muslims and Arabs, while the Christians used mostly Latin, and the Jews both Hebrew and Arabic.

The flowering of Andalusian culture was to a great extent the result of the positive interaction of diverse peoples, refreshed with a continuous ebb and flow of new people, ideas and languages, all pointing towards submission to God along the path of Islam.

The expulsion of Muslims from Andalusia and the subsequent persecution of all faiths other than the official Catholic dogma resulted in the cultural immobilization of Spain from the seventeenth century onwards. Spain had been the pivot of cultural, economic and spiritual exchange between the thriving world of Islam and the emerging European civilization. The Renaissance was fuelled by the wealth of knowledge and skills that poured into Europe through the conduit of Muslim Andalusia. But by the mid-sixteenth century the healthy interaction and cross-fertilization of ideas, scholarship and creative thought was brought to a complete halt. This ended eight centuries in which great advances in human civilization were shared openly in Spain.

INTERNATIONAL ISLAM AND INDEPENDENT SULTANS (945–1258)

By the tenth century the Abbasid caliphate was already disintegrating, and the world of Islam was no longer contained as a single political unit. Muslims at this time could be divided into three general geographical areas. One area was the land of Iran, southern Mesopotamia and the lands beyond the Oxus (Transoxiana). These were ruled by the central power in Baghdad. Another area included Egypt, Syria and western Arabia, with the centre of power located in the Fatimid City of Cairo. The third area included North Africa, the Maghreb and Andalus.

Whilst the Abbasids' political and administrative ability to keep a framework of unity waned, Islam, with its numerous cultural and theological variations, emerged as the real but subtly diffused unifying force for the Muslims. Conviction and belief in one God, and attempts to adhere to the prophetic teachings and conduct re-emerged as the basis for stable relationships among the numerous Muslims. Their common religion and existential behaviour were given expression in the Arabic language in most of the western parts, while both Arabic and Persian were used in the east.

During the tenth century a new kind of Persian language (written in the Arabic script) began to emerge from the old Pahlavi. Although based on Pahlavi, it was greatly enriched by Arabic vocabulary. This development effectively marked a major departure in the culture and civilization of the Muslims, for previously it had been based exclusively on the Arabic language and, therefore, on the relatively unchanged habits of the Arabs.

From the tenth century to the sixteenth, the political trend moved towards increasingly decentralized power. In Egypt and Syria the Ikhshidids (of Turkish origin) established an independent dynasty (935–969). The Fatimids, who had already established themselves in Tunis in 909, captured Egypt in 969, built Cairo and the al-Azhar mosque and university. They continued to rule until 1171, when they were replaced by Saladin (1169–1193), a military leader of Kurdish origin who managed to mobilize religious fervour in Egypt and Syria in order to defeat the Crusaders who had established a Christian state in Palestine and on the Syrian coast at the end of the eleventh century. The dynasty he founded, known as the Ayyubids, ruled from 1169–1252, in Syria until 1260 and parts of western Arabia until 1229.

The Hamdanis (Shi'i Arab tribesmen) established their rule over Mosul and Aleppo, patronizing such luminaries as the philosopher al-Farabi (d.950) and the poet Al-Mutanabbi (d.965). In Baghdad the Buyids, from the mountain of Daylam, had taken power in 930.

Persia rose in importance as a centre for trade and culture. The Samanids (874–999) ruled in Khurasan and Transoxiana, including Rayy and Kerman. Their capital was Bukhara, the second most important city being Samarqand. Persian literature's renaissance reached fresh heights based on the new language. Ibn Sina (Avicenna, d.1037), Ferdawsi (d.1020), and others such as al-Razi (Rhazes) and Rudaki are among the many outstanding figures who contributed enormously to Muslim civilization, and whose impact remained for many centuries to follow.

When the central Samanid family lost control to military chiefs, their lands were divided from 990 onwards between the Ghaznavids and Karakhanids, which is when Seljuq rule began. The Seljuqs were nomads descended from Turkoman and Khwarazm Shah. In 1030 they defeated the Ghaznavids and in 1040 divided up the territory amongst their ruling families. In 1055 the Togruqs and Seljuqs were in Baghdad. The Vizier to Malik Shah built an Islamic university there, the famous Nizamiyyah Madrasah (established in 1065), as well as an extensive network of agricultural towns, roads, markets and mosques. By 1091 the Seljuqs had firmly established their capital at Baghdad.

Muhammad Ghaznavi (998–1030) was the most prominent ruler of this period at Ghazni in the Afghan Mountains, and it was to his court that Ferdawsi brought the Shahnameh, an epic recounting the story of the old Persian monarchs.

When the Crusaders took Jerusalem in 1099, the weakened Seljuqs did not move to its defence. By 1118 their kingdom had broken up into principalities in Khurasan (lasting until 1157), and in Anatolia (lasting until 1307).

By the tenth century the social system was such that a Muslim of whatever origin could take his place in society entirely on the basis of his merits and thereby attain a position which accorded with the quality of his character, piety and behaviour. Many persons of humble origin rose high in political stature, exercising considerable influence over the local rulers and within their governments.

For the next hundred and fifty years from the mid-tenth century, Persian literature and culture developed rapidly, paralleled by a significant rise in the number of Muslim philosophers and theologians. Imam Ghazali tried to harmonize Sufism with Sunni teachings, and in Andalusia Ibn Bajjah the philosopher-physician (d.1138) popularized the knowledge of the union between the soul and the Divine. Ibn Tufayl, the Anadalusian philosopher-physician, authored the tale *Hayy Ibn Yaqzan* (Alive, son of the awakened), 'awakened' that is, by the natural processes of interacting with nature, reasoning, reflecting and ultimately being enlightened. The story is an example of the illuminist philosophy of Ibn Sina. Ibn Rushd (Averroes, d.1198), another Andalusian philosopher-physician-cum-jurist, propagated and popularized Aristotelian philosophy. Other notable figures of the time include the philosopher Fakhr al-Din al-Razi (d.1209) and the great philosopher-astronomer Nasir al-Din al-Tusi (d.1274).

THE CRUSADES

The Crusades of the Middle East were medieval Christian military expeditions undertaken between 1095 and 1291 to 'recover' the Holy Lands from the Muslims. There were eight major Crusades and some minor, peripheral military excursions.

The idea of the Crusades was born in Spain. The battle of Poitiers and many others were the precursors to what later came to be called the Crusades (see pages 90–7). From the ninth century fear of Islam and the need to counteract its spread became a serious concern for the Roman Papacy. With the weakening of centralized rule in Spain during the tenth and eleventh centuries, the Christian principalities were encouraged by the Pope and his emissaries to expand by any and every means. The rapid spread of Islam into the European side of the Mediterranean (including Malta, Sicily and Sardinia) had built up to a point where the Papacy realized that unless it checked Islam effectively, its own years were numbered.

The Arabs had conquered Jerusalem in 638 under the Caliph 'Umar, who treated the Christian inhabitants justly and with respect. By the mid-eleventh century Jerusalem was a prosperous and cosmopolitan centre, but the Seljuq conquests of Byzantine territories had made it unsafe for Christian pilgrims. The Emperor Alexius Comnenus appealed for military aid from the West, and Pope Urban II responded with the call to the First Crusade in 1095. This Crusade served to divert the energy of the belligerent nobles of north-western Europe, as well as spur on the peasantry with the possibility of finding their fortune in distant lands. Also, the Second Coming of Jesus was only possible if Jerusalem were in Christian hands.

Peter the Hermit, a preacher from Germany, led the first army, called the 'People's Crusade', into Constantinople, where they caused great disturbance. Almost their entire force was massacred by the Turks.

Another crusading army entered Jerusalem in July 1099 and massacred a great number of Muslims and Jews. They attempted to force the practices of the Latin Church upon the eastern Christians by torturing the Orthodox priests. In contrast to this, while it had been under Muslim rule the Church of the Holy Sepulchre had been allowed to retain altars belonging to all the oriental Christian sects. Godfrey of Bouillon was recognized as the governor of Jerusalem, and upon his death his brother Baldwin came from Antioch and was crowned King of Jerusalem in 1100. Under him a feudal kingdom emerged.

In 1145 Zangi, the governor of Mosul, led a *Jihad* and captured Odessa, with the result that a second Crusade, led by Louis VII of France, was launched. This culminated in defeat in the unsuccessful siege of Damascus which failed due to lack of co-operation from the Byzantine Emperor Manuel. This propelled Louis VII to plot a Crusade against Byzantium with the help of Roger of Sicily, but this came to nothing.

Twenty-five years on, the kingdom of Jerusalem was in the hands of Nureddin (Zangi's son). While he occupied Damascus, by 1196 his deputy controlled Egypt in his name. Saladin went on to occupy Aleppo, and when the Christians broke their truce with him he destroyed most of Jerusalem's army at Hittin near the Sea of Galilee. His capture of Jerusalem precipitated the Third Crusade (the largest of them all), which was led by the Emperor Frederick Barbarossa of Germany

101

in 1189. In 1191 Richard the Lionheart took Cyprus. He never reached Jerusalem, but in 1192 managed to negotiate a five-year peace treaty with Saladin which gave pilgrims access to the shrines.

The Fourth Crusade to attack the Muslims of Egypt in 1198 was called by Pope Innocent III, but the Crusaders, unable to pay the Venetians for their ships, were diverted into helping them attack Constantinople, which fell to them in 1204. This move destroyed any possibility of co-operation between the Eastern and Western Churches.

The Children's Crusade of 1212, in which thousands of children were killed or sold into slavery, was undoubtedly the most shameful of them all.

In 1219 the Fifth Crusade, led by the French and Germans, captured Dammietta near the Nile and an eight-year truce was arranged. In 1229, Emperor Frederick II negotiated a treaty by peaceful means which returned Jerusalem to the Europeans for ten years. King Louis IX of France led the Seventh Crusade to Egypt in 1248 as well as the Eighth to North Africa in 1270, during which he died in Tunis.

The Crusader Kings of Jerusalem gave rise to two powerful religio-military orders: the Hospitallers, who provided hospital care for pilgrims, and the Knights Templar, whose job it was to protect pilgrims on their way. These knights were a law unto themselves and their influence was as great as the wealth they accumulated through properties in the East and Europe. Their activities, which were shrouded in secrecy, included peculiar rites of initiation, and their connection with the Isma'ili Assassins suggest the influence of the esoteric teachings of Islam, albeit in a distorted form. Accusing them of heresy and immorality, Philip IV of France persuaded Pope Clement V to suppress them in 1312. Two years later their leader Jacques de Molay was burnt at the stake. Present-day Freemasons are said by some to be their heirs.

The Crusades had been launched to save Eastern Christendom from the Muslims, yet by the time they ended the East was entirely under Muslim Ottoman rule. The Crusades had enhanced the power and prestige of the Papacy at the cost of the various Eastern Christian minority sects, but it also displaced the strong nobles, allowing monarchical power to rise.

The oriental Christian sects had enjoyed greater freedom of worship under Muslim than Latin Christian rule. The barbarous behaviour of the Christians – as evinced by their massacre of surrendering armies – lost them the tolerance of the Muslims, who were to retaliate in later years with equal levels of savagery and persecution. The Franks who settled in the East learned to interact with the locals and so benefited from their higher standard of living. Returning Crusaders brought home with them the experience of comforts of living in regular bathing, food and dress, then unknown to their countrymen. However, it was through Spain and Sicily that real access to the civilizing aspects of Muslim culture filtered into Europe.

MONGOLS, MUGHALS AND OTHER DYNASTIES (1258–1503)

The first great Mongol raids were launched around 1220–1231 in Azerbaijan and north-east Iran, causing enormous destruction to cities. Ghengis Khan (d.1127) and his heirs continued their conquests and expansion until by 1256 the Mongols had devastated and brought under their rule most Iranian and Arab lands, except the Ayyubids in Egypt and the Seljuqs in Anatolia.

Ironically, the same Mongols who ruled over Iran from 1256 and destroyed much of Baghdad in 1258 were converted to Islam in 1295 and brought renewed vitality to the Muslims. Soon after their conversion they patronized science, history and art forms inspired by other segments of Eurasian society including, among others, pagan, Buddhist and Christian.

The Golden Horde Mongols north of the Caspian and the Black Seas (called the *Kipchak*) were also converted to Islam and remained in control of those areas until the Russian conquest during the sixteenth century.

Timur Lang revived Mongol power in Samarqand (1369–1405) and conquered and ransacked various towns in the Middle East and central Asia, sacking Delhi in 1398. Between 1405 and 1494 the Timurids in Khurasan and Transoxiana fostered science, and Persian and Turkic literature, and developed miniature painting to a very fine art. Ulugh Beg (1393–1449), the Timurid ruler at Samarqand, patronized research and astronomy, causing them also to flourish.

The Mongols were defeated at 'Ain Jalut in 1260 by the Mamluk Sultan Baybars, who then overcame the Frankish power on the Syrian coast (1260–1277). Qal'un (1280–1290) completed the elimination of the Franks from Syria and established a dynasty that lasted until 1382.

Among the great men of Islam of the era were Jalal al-Din Rumi (d.1273), Nasir al-Din al-Tusi (d.1274), Sa'di (d.1257), and Hafiz (d.1390).

By the thirteenth century numerous Turkic tribes established independence from the Seljuqs and their Mongol overlords. Erteghul, the father of Othman, founder of the Ottoman dynasty, was one such small ruler in the Anatolian plateau. 'Uthman (1288–1326) made his corner of the Anatolian Seljuq state a military centre, and by 1288 the Ottoman dynasty there and in the Balkans was expanding over Slav and Greek territory.

Murad I (1359–1389) took Adrianople (which became the capital) and defeated the Balkan Christians at Kossovo in 1389, thereby dominating most of the Balkan peninsula as well as western Anatolia.

Between 1384 and 1402 Bayazid I expanded Ottoman power in Anatolia but was defeated by Timur. In 1403 Mehmed I gradually reunited the shattered Empire, to be succeeded by Murad II, who asserted his power into Hungary. Murad II captured Constantinople in 1453. The Ottomans took Rhodes in 1522 and Cyprus in 1570.

During this latter period of expansion and conquest Islam exercised a considerable civilizing influence over numerous nations stretching from China to eastern Europe, the Atlantic, North Africa and Spain. However, along with these achievements came examples of oppression, despotism and greed.

Mehmed II (1451–1481) took Constantinople (called Islambul but later changed to Istanbul), which became his capital. He encouraged the assimilation of Byzantine cultural tradition and learning, an attitude continued by his son Bayazid II (1481–1512).

During the fifteenth and sixteenth centuries Muslim countries faced a new challenge from the states of western Europe.

We notice the beginning of the reversal of a trend in trade and production that had been sustained for centuries. Manufacture of textiles and other goods in European cities grew, and the merchants from Venice and Genoa increased their exports to the Muslim world. The extinction of the Sultanate of Granada in 1492 and the subsequent Spanish and Portuguese expansion into the New World and elsewhere brought about new threats. The extensive use of gunpowder helped to usher in changes more swiftly, as well as prolonging and expanding certain dynasties. An example of this is 'Uthman's defeat of the Mamluks in the early sixteenth century, which absorbed Syria and Egypt as well as western Arabia into the Empire (1516–1517). The Ottoman Empire survived until 1924.

The Islamic code of conduct – with spiritual awakening as its ultimate goal – and its resulting cultural and civilizing influences continued to be the main source for human development throughout the known world, until the fall of Granada. This fall signified a break in contact and interaction between Muslims and Christians in western Europe. Within a century or so, Western supremacy – military, political, commercial, industrial, technological and monetaristic – was being realized, often at the expense and to the detriment of the rest of the world.

NATIONAL EMPIRES AND THE SHIFT IN POWER

From the time of the Mongol conquest of Baghdad until the early sixteenth century, we can discern a pattern of regular rises and falls of small and large kingdoms, or varying ethnicities and depth of commitment to original Islam. By the sixteenth century the socio-political map displayed three distinct areas:

- The Ottoman Empire (fully established 1514–1922)
- The Mughal Empire (1526–1763)
- The Safavid Empire and its successors in Iran (1502–1773)

THE OTTOMAN EMPIRE UNTIL 1789

Sultan Selim I (1512–1520) expanded his power into Azerbaijan, where he suppressed all Shi'i and other dissident movements.

He conquered Egypt in 1517, defeating the Mamluks, and established his reign in west Arabia, thereby controlling the pilgrimage centre of Islam. During the reign of Sulayman the Magnificent (1520–1566) the Ottoman Empire was substantially consolidated and enlarged. Rhodes was taken in 1520, Vienna was besieged in 1529, and Hungary was ruled directly from 1541.

Under Sultan Selim II and Murad II (1566–1595) there was a move towards peace abroad and a relaxation of institutional bureaucracy at home. Great mosques were built, such as the Sulaymaniyah in Istanbul and the Selimiyah in Idirne, sponsored by Selim and Murad and built by the great architect Sinan Pasha (d.1578).

The Janissary corps had by now become too powerful but was subdued by Murad IV (1623–1640). Decline of military as well as institutional efficiency led to the first major military setbacks in Europe with the defeat at Vienna and the loss of Hungary and Belgrade during the latter part of the seventeenth century. In 1718 the Ottomans experienced their second major defeat, at the hands of the Hapsburgs. With the help of his influential vizier, Ibrahim Pasha, Sultan Ahmad III attempted major westernization and reform (the printing press was introduced in 1726). Although Mustafa II was known for his desire for peace, he became embroiled in war with Russia, and faced the total defeat of his armies and the loss of the Crimea in 1774. The victorious Tsar was declared the protector of the Christians in Ottoman lands.

Selim III (1789–1807) embarked on fresh waves of a westernizing type of reform, establishing Ottoman embassies in European capitals, and imitating Western-style bureaucratic institutions. There was little mass support or participation, and these alien practices did not take root. Having enjoyed considerable military and cultural superiority up to the sixteenth century, the Ottoman Empire's collapse at the hands of the Russians was total.

THE TIMURID EMPIRE (until 1763)

The Indian Timurid Empire commenced with Babar. He was driven from his Timurid state to Farghanah and after re-establishing his power in Kabul took north India. He was succeeded by Humayun Sher Shah and Akbar (1556–1605). As the third Mughal Emperor, Akbar fostered Hindu-Muslim cultural and religious rapprochement, which caused the arts and crafts to flourish. Court scholars and historians elevated Akbar to the status of 'Perfect Man'.

Jehangir (1605–1627) and Shah Jehan (1628–1658), who built the Taj Mahal at Agra, continued Akbar's policy of promoting art, portraiture and architecture, reaching a high state of refinement. Ahmed Sirhindi (d.1625) sparked off a new wave of Islamic reform and anti-Akbarism in the hope of awakening the Muslim masses to true Islamic conduct.

Aurangzeb (1658–1707), the last of the great Mughals, reversed the policy of co-operation with the Hindus, enforcing orthodox Sunni Islam wherever he could. Bahadur tried to arrest the decay of the Empire (1707–1712), but by 1720 the Mughal Empire had lost its southern and eastern provinces, maintaining only weak and largely ceremonial political control.

Nadir Shah sacked Delhi in 1739 and brought what remained of Mughal imperial power in India to an end. In 1762 Shah Wali Ullah, a great Sufi reformer, undertook a rapprochement between the upholders of the *Shari'ah* of Islam and the supporters of the Sirhindi ideas. A year later, having defeated the French in the Seven Years War, the British expanded their control over the disunited Indian states.

THE SAFAVID EMPIRE AND ITS SUCCESSORS (1509–1779)

Shah Isma'il Safavi (1502–1524) built up a Turko-Persian Shi'i empire in Iran, suppressing most Sufi orders (although his own ancestors had been Sufis), and persecuting Sunnis. Shah 'Abbas the Great (1587–1629) expanded the Empire, driving the Ottomans out of Azerbaijan in Iran, and built the great city of Isfahan.

The first half of the seventeenth century saw a considerable religious revival of spiritual and philosophical activity, for stability and prosperity had created a healthy ambience for the development of spiritual teachings, as evinced by the establishment of the Islamic School of Metaphysics near Byzance in 1630. It was during this time that the transcendent work of the philosopher and theologian Mulla Sadra (d.1640) took shape.

The Empire remained in prosperous peace until the reign of Husayn Shah (1672–1722), which was undermined by the Afghan revolt, the capture of Isfahan and the massacre of the Persian nobility. In 1779 the Qajar dynasty was founded by Muhammad Agha Khan after thirty years of civil war among the various Turkish tribes clamouring to rule.

Having come into being with a significant flourish of culture, the Safavid Empire ended in an extremely weakened state, sandwiched between the Russians to the north and the British to the east and west. Although Nadir Shah had conquered Delhi in 1739, this was only a prelude to the British gaining control over India from 1747 onwards.

THE SHIFT IN POWER

Between 1500 and 1800 (and in particular after 1600) the power of the Christian Churches dwindled and the secular 'rational' European powers came to dominate the world from the French Revolution onwards. The interaction with the Muslim world during the fourteenth to sixteenth centuries (mostly via Spain) formed the background to the Renaissance of Europe and the subsequent discovery and conquest of the New World. The dynamic momentum of European awakening, laced with Christian dogma and intensive national competition and greed, spilled over into the plunder of new territories. The discovery of America, circumnavigation of the world, and the wealth that was brought back to Europe fuelled early commercial and later industrial development which led to the industrial dominance of Europe in the eighteenth century.

Up until 1500 no European city was more advanced than any of the major cities in the Muslim world. However, by 1650 the story was very different. In most matters of commercial, industrial and organizational significance Europe had advanced. In military matters, for example, the Ottomans and others depended on arms, technicians, engineers and businessmen imported from Europe. Even the printing press, which had been available from as early as the sixteenth century (owned mostly by Jews expelled from Europe) was not used by Muslims until the early nineteenth century. What Muslims lacked was the infrastructure, discipline and organization to maintain and develop basic technology that depended on the people rather than on the patronage of the ruler.

European competition for raw materials had met with the relative tolerance and often Western orientation of Muslim rulers. This allowed them to increase their strength and enabled them to infiltrate Muslim lands. Many Muslim rulers were infatuated with Western products, gadgets, style and fashion, but lacked the willingness (or understanding of the need) to develop from their own grass roots an equivalent Islamic alternative. They preferred to transplant without developing the appropriate infrastructure and practices to absorb these new products and technologies in a way that was harmonious with Islamic conduct.

By the seventeenth century Europe had come to dominate in commerce, trade, industry and technology, as well as military and organizational affairs. Its marked competitive drive, spurred no doubt in part by the need to conquer the harshness of their colder climates in order to survive, expanded their control. It is at this time that we witness the integration of these areas with the educational, political, financial and social life in all European countries. Well in place by now were the creation and establishment of a civil service, the beginnings of liberal democracies, and the limitation of the power of the monarchy and other nobility. In all such civic matters the Muslims lagged behind.

The shift in the balance of strength in trade, industry, warfare, technology and so on to Europe was witnessed everywhere in Muslim lands. The seeds of this change can be traced back at least two hundred years from the early sixteenth century, when Muslims (and Jews) had been expelled from Spain. Their banishment marked the end of open and natural exchange between the Muslims and Europe. This breakdown in the interactive relationship between Muslims and Christians lay at the root of the subsequent deprivation of Muslims, preventing them from benefiting from the material advancement of Europe. As a result the European imperial powers were able to overtake and exploit not only the Muslims but the rest of the world. With Napoleon's entry into Egypt in 1798 and total British control of the sub-continent and Middle East, European worldly prowess was supreme.

THE NINETEENTH AND TWENTIETH CENTURIES: EUROPEAN TECHNO-ECONOMICAL CONTROL

To understand the overwhelming power and influence the West acquired within Muslim lands, we need to look at four Muslim political entities: the Ottoman Empire, Egypt, Iran and India.

THE OTTOMAN EMPIRE

Mahmud II (1808–1839) exercised greater centralized control when he modernized the military and administration and destroyed the Janissaries. The European powers then stepped in to save the Ottomans from Mehmed 'Ali of Egypt who was about to overrun them. This protection earned them all the mercantile concessions giving them virtual control over the Ottoman Empire.

Sultan Abdul Mejid (1839–1861) inaugurated overt westernizing reforms to restore 'the sick man of Europe', and total Western hegemony was completed during the reign of Sultan 'Abdul Aziz (1861–1876), when he drove the Empire into bankruptcy. The huge loans he had taken from Western banks gave European governments and their bankers control of the entire fabric of the Empire's finances under the misleadingly named Ottoman National Public Debt Administration (misleading because it was not an Ottoman creation, and neither was the Ottoman Bank, which was controlled by the French and other Europeans). In just under a decade the Western banks' ultimate financial conquest and exploitation was repeated throughout the remaining Muslim lands. So-called Islamic modernist movements and subsequent Islamic apology, compromise of values, and other emotional sentiments and frustration, all helped Western techno-usurious institutions to establish legal dominance in Muslim lands, camouflaged with a local flavour.

110

In 1865 the Young Ottoman Society (the Young Turks) popularized patriotism and constitutionalism. There then followed more than thirty years of palace revolutions and other attempts to create a constitution, culminating with the Turko-Greek War of 1896–1897. Sultan 'Abdul Hamid's attempts to restore Islamic value and dignity and his Pan-Islamic movement was to no avail. In 1909 the Sultan restored the constitution only to face revolt. He was deposed in favour of Muhammad V, who entered the First World War, was defeated, and left the country in greater disarray and breakdown.

Mustafa Kemal (Ataturk) emerged from the War of Independence (1919–1922) as a national hero, only to abolish the caliphate and Shari'ah Courts. A year later he also abolished the Sufi tariqahs and the fez. This led in 1928 to the disestablishment of Islam, the introduction of the Latin alphabet, and European rimmed hats to replace the fez (one cannot perform the prayers with such headgear as the width of the rim prevents prostration and no self-respecting Muslim would pray without a headcover). By 1947 Turkey had become a hostage state indebted to the Western banking and political systems.

From 1950 onwards Turkey appeared to embrace democracy geared by a Western-controlled army to ensure timely payment of debts and check excessive political ambitions from zealous politicians. The course of westernization at all costs became the national and political agenda of all leaders with the aim of being admitted to the exclusive European Club, the EEC, glimmering hopefully on the horizon.

EGYPT

The cultural and material impact caused by Napoleon's occupation of Egypt on the élite of Egyptian society drew them towards the French way of life and culture. By 1805 Mehmed 'Ali started his ambitious programme of modernization and westernization. In 1816 he confiscated trust (waqf) properties, and sent numerous educational missions to Europe. His powerful ambitions were being realized so rapidly that when he almost overtook the Ottomans in Turkey, the European powers forced him to withdraw and eventually dismantled his industrial complexes, for they threatened to undermine the predominance of his Western masters' industries.

Khedive Sa'id (1854–1863) attempted to develop Egypt's agriculture and industry, but ended immersed in foreign debt under European mercantile domination. His successor, Isma'il, embarked on a futile project to transform Egypt into a part of Europe. The cotton boom (due to the American Civil War), the opening of the Suez Canal in 1869, and later excessive European loans resulted in the sale of the Canal to the British in 1875 and increased indebtedness to Western banks. In order to ensure repayment of these hugh loans, total legal control of Egyptian finances was gained in 1876.

Subsequent attempts to revitalize the Muslims, such as the 'Arabi Mutiny, al-Afghani and 'Abduh's modernism, and others, eventually led to full British military occupation. Lord Cromer established a Western-style administration with certain allowances made for nationalism that lasted until the First World War, when Egypt was declared a protectorate. In 1922 Egypt was granted formal independence with British control over defence, foreign policy, economic and military matters.

The defeat of the Arabs in Palestine in 1948 and the ineptitude and decadence of the royal family (under King Faruq) led to the Officers' Revolt in 1952. This was the first time ever that Egypt was ruled by a native Egyptian, Gamal 'Abdul Nasser. Subsequent Arab nationalism and dreams of Arab unity dictated from the top have driven the country even further into external political and military confrontation, disagreement and internal impoverishment. President Sadat embraced the Zionists in the hope of a miracle cure, and his successor maintains control through American back-up. Since then Egypt's basket economy has been under the supervision of the IMF and American aid. Political leadership is constantly on the lookout for Western favours and acknowledgement of service. Several billion dollars of Egyptian debt were thus 'forgiven' thanks to effective Egyptian participation on the side of the Americans in their recent war with Iraq.

IRAN

European influence and rivalry between the British and Russians date from the time of Fath 'Ali Shah (1767–1834). Caucasia was ceded to Russia, and other central Asian territories were taken over. Nasiruddin Shah (1848–1896), infatuated with Europe and Britain, had by 1857 granted them significant concessions. In 1872 commercial and monetaristic capitulation was completed when Baron de Reuters was granted monopolistic concessions on banking and mining. The Shah's assassination in 1896 was followed by great unrest and frustration. In 1901 oil was discovered and the country occupied by Britain and Russia, who appointed Reza Khan as head of a Turkish-style secular republic (or Shahdom) in 1925.

Reza Shah brutally transplanted a westernizing style of government (imitating Ataturk). His despotic laws on dress and religion did not save him from being deposed in 1941 by the British and Russians, for by then he had begun to believe in the myth of his independence.

The last attempts to gain a certain measure of independence under Mosaddeq (1951–1953) subsequently led to far greater dependence on Western technology and training for the oil industry. Continuing headlong Americanization by the second Reza Shah resulted in the Revolution of 1979 and his exile. Imam Khomeini's personal piety and uncompromising basic Islamic faith and conduct set numerous waves of revival into motion within Iran and beyond. The rise of Khomeini should be understood as an early signpost of Islamic revival to come. He was a great symbolic product of it, not a cause.

INDIA

Britain had established its hegemony over India by 1818 through conquest or treaty, and occupied the remaining Indus Basin by 1849. The war against the British between 1857 and 1858 resulted in considerable anti-Muslim discrimination, producing such modernists as Sir Seyyed Ahmad Khan who loyally advocated adapting British culture to Shari'ah law.

India remained under total British control until the Second World War, after which it was divided into one secular state

(India), and another (Pakistan) which aspired towards establishing Islam as its *raison d'être*, whilst living on subsidies and controls from the West, and the US in particular (the local agent being Saudi Arabia).

SUMMARY

By the middle of the twentieth century, Western-inspired modernizing movements were rampant all over Muslim lands. The pattern subscribed to was to emulate Western socio-economic democracies, mainly along the lines of republics and multi-party systems. By the time Israel was created in 1948 the Muslim peoples had been broken up into dozens of states, protectorates and emirates. Occasional feeble attempts to enforce *Shari'ah* laws erupted here and there, but no revival of Islamic values has changed the basic status quo.

By the middle of this century all Muslim territories had been brought firmly into the grip of the invisible mercantile controls of the Western (and latterly Japanese) multi-national, multi-faceted financial services with their headquarters in Wall Street, London, Tokyo and Frankfurt. The ultimate objective of most of the fragmented national governments has been to maximize short-term economic (and often military) gains in order to anaesthetize their people and thus maintain control. By 1990 over forty so-called Muslim states found it impossible to meet and agree on any vital political or economic issue affecting their so-called sovereign states, or the world at large.

MUSLIMS WITHIN THE SOVIET EMPIRE

In 639 Arab Muslims entered Azerbaijan and within three years occupied Daghestan. In 673 the Muslims crossed the Amu Darya river and laid siege to Bukhara. By the early eighth century Islam had become the dominant religion in all this territory. Between the ninth and thirteenth centuries Islam spread peacefully along the north – south trade routes along the Volga (the fur route), as well as east – west from the Black Sea to China (the silk road). By the tenth century Middle Volga (present-day Tartar territory) was predominantly

Muslim, as were the Urals by the twelfth. Until the end of the sixteenth century central Asia was one of the most prestigious cultural and spiritual areas of the entire Muslim world.

From central Asia Muslim merchants – Arabs, Iranians and Turks – brought Islam to the Kazaq steppes, north of the Kirghiz mountains and finally to eastern Turkestan (present-day Xianging).

During the early thirteenth century Mongol rule was anti-Islamic in character because of the Buddhist and Nestorian Christian influences among the leaders. However, because of Sufi brotherhoods Islam survived and became rooted in the populace. The Sufi masters and missionaries, in addition to the traders and merchants, played a crucial role in expanding Islam until it was embraced by the Mongols.

It is interesting to note that apart from the Spaniards and the people of the Balkans, the Russians were the only Christian nation in Europe to have experienced such a long history of Muslim establishment and rule. By the mid-sixteenth century the centralized Muscovite State had driven back the weakened Golden Horde heirs and conquered most of the important Muslim territories, such as Kazan in 1552, Astrakhan in 1556, and western Siberia in 1598. By the end of the seventeenth century the Russians had reached the north Caucasus. As they systematically occupied Muslim lands they established a network of fortresses for their exclusive military use and subsequent settlement. Ivan the Terrible then annexed all Muslim territories. From now on the Muslim nobility was faced with either converting to Christianity or total economic servitude. Those who resisted were destroyed. Muslim leaders were expelled from the cities, their mosques destroyed and the masses were to a great extent forcibly converted.

Paradoxically, the spread of Islam under the Russian Empire throughout the eighteenth century was not impeded by Russian domination. However, during Catherine II's reign (she held Islam in high regard) the name of the Ottoman Sultan continued to be mentioned every Friday prayers in all the Crimean mosques. In 1782 Catherine created an Islamic assembly, chaired by a Mufti nominated by the Imperial Minister of the Interior so as to increase centralized control. The appearance of the Naqshbandi Sufi missionaries by the end of the eighteenth century in the north Caucasus heralded a new expansion under Russian rule. The Qadiriyah order also appeared during the nineteenth century and established numerous centres in the north Caucasus.

In 1855 the Russians embarked upon the conquest of central Asia in earnest. With the exception of Khiva and Bukhara, central Asia was placed under the military administration of the Governor General of Turkestan. Native Muslims were not considered to be citizens of the Empire. Russian policy towards the Muslims of this vast region was a classically imperial one. They neither attempted to russify the natives, nor did they introduce any improvements. They isolated the Muslims while patronizing a formal and ritualistic version of Islam, meanwhile extracting great quantities of raw materials, minerals and other primary agricultural produce from their lands.

When the decree of 1905 was published announcing religious liberty in Russia, Islam entered a new phase of revival and growth when the majority of Muslim Tartars, who had been forcibly converted to Christianity in the eighteenth and nineteenth centuries, returned to their old faith. However, official disapproval of religious activities and disdain towards Muslims continued. *Madrasahs* were closed, religious endowments liquidated, and all religious courts suppressed.

From 1928 to 1941 there was a frontal assault on Islam within the Soviet borders. In 1912 the official census had quoted 26,279 mosques, but, according to government sources, there were no more than 1,500 by 1958.

Krushchev continued the anti-Islamic policies of his predecessors, even accusing Islam of being the main cause of the many social ills of Russia, and Gorbachev picked up the suppressive policies of Krushchev towards Islam. The campaign to contain and oppress the Muslims has been temporarily restrained in 1964 when Brezhnev came to power and found the Muslim presence a useful instrument in his diplomatic policies in the Middle East.

The dynamic unofficial Islam in the former Soviet Union is mostly based upon the Sufi networks, in particular the Naqshbandi and the Qadiri. Both these *Tariqahs* have a long history of Holy Wars against the Russian conquerors. Shaykh

Shamil in the nineteenth century, Imam Najmuddin of Godsaw and Shaykh Uzul al-Hajj, who led the great Daghestani revolt in 1920, were among the many great *mujahids*. The Qadiris were behind the anti-Communist movement which broke out in the Chechen territory in 1942.

The Soviet Empire's attempts to contain and suppress the growth of Islamic sentiment and revival during this century included patronizing a centrally organized official Islam. Ironically this in no way defused the Islamic awakening that had been penetrating the growing underground networks of Muslims. With the break-up of the USSR, the inevitably greater freedom and autonomy that will be enjoyed in the various republics will invigorate the Muslims and accelerate the revival of Islam.

MUSLIMS ELSEWHERE

Since the dawn of Islam numerous Muslim communities and nations have sprung up in Africa, Asia, Europe and elsewhere. A few examples are given below.

As early as 758 a few Muslims had settled in Chinese ports, and Muslim traders soon established outposts in many of the other ports in south-east Asia. Numerous pockets of Muslims began to appear in most of this area's regions without any visible political impact until the thirteenth century.

By the end of the thirteenth century many Muslims were residing in the Sumatran ports, maintaining strong and close contacts with other trading posts and the Gujarat Muslims. By the fourteenth century the ruler of Malacca had converted to Islam, and the city became an important entryport to China for the Indian Ocean trade, and for spreading Islam through the southern Malay peninsula and the neighbouring islands. By the sixteenth century, the Portuguese had come to dominate the Indian Ocean trade. Having defeated the Egyptian Mamluks in Gujarat in 1509, they then beat the Ottoman Gujarati forces in 1538. In 1507 Sultan 'Ali established his kingdom in northern Sumatra, and in 1518 the Hindu Kingdom of East Java was replaced by Muslim rule. Today sizeable Muslim populations are still to be found in Malaysia, Indonesia and the Philippines.

By the eleventh century Islam had arrived in the Sudanese lands of North Africa through trade, and the Almoravids established their centres in Mauritania. By the thirteenth century the Ghana Empire had collapsed and the rulers of the Lake Chad area were converted to Islam, bound by strong religious and trade links with Egypt and North Africa. In 1324 the King of gold-rich Mali performed the pilgrimage to Mecca in grand style, and regular caravans plied back and forth to the Maghreb and Egypt. By the fourteenth century Mali, Timbuctu and Gao had become important Muslim centres. By the end of the fifteenth century the Mali Empire fell, but the central Sudan Empire rose and the Hausa predominated in eastern Niger (1517–1801). In 1698 the resurgent *Kharijis* drove the Portuguese from Zanzibar and established Muslim cities and centres in East Africa and Muscat.

Elsewhere in Africa numerous Muslim principalities and kingdoms come into being in West as well as East Africa. Tribal conversions have continued until the present day in spite of disapproval from Western-influenced governments and agencies.

There were numerous small communities of Muslims all over the world, even including some early Africans taken as slaves to America. There were large numbers of Muslims, mostly from Arab lands, among the early immigrants to South America (President Menem's father was a Syrian), and many pockets of Muslims still exist in many central and South American countries. Muslims lived in eastern Europe as far north as Switzerland where even today there are villages with Muslim names. Large numbers of Yugoslavians, Bulgarians and Albanians are Muslim to this day, but sadly through the years of isolation, many of those Muslims who migrated have lost much of their cultural and religious identity.

6 · THE LIFE OF MUSLIMS

The faith of Islam is founded on the belief that there is One Compassionate, All-encompassing God; that the purpose of His creation is to know Him; and that the approved existential behaviour is sustained only in order to arrive at that knowledge. Man's primary and most urgent business is the knowledge of God, and the transformation that naturally follows. Every other human pursuit is secondary.

In this chapter we look at how Islam transformed people's outlook on life and how it shaped the way they lived. What were the unifying factors that gave Muslim culture its cohesion? How did Islam affect business and trade? What was the relationship between rulers and the ruled, and why was it that they did not produce a stable 'civil service' independent of the ruler's person? These and other questions are addressed by focusing on specific aspects of the life of Muslims, which because of limitations of space is by no means comprehensive.

As a complete system of life-transaction the *Din* of Islam affects every aspect of human experience. It permeates the person at the physical, material, mental, intellectual and spiritual levels, and therefore percolates into individual, familial, social and every other aspect of civil and cultural life. It is for this reason that we find such strong symmetry amongst racially, culturally and geographically diverse Muslims. A familiar thread weaves its way visibly from the life of a Muslim in China to the life of a Muslim in West Africa. There always

119

have been and always will be localized elements of indigenous custom and cultural expression, but this diversity reflects geographically inherent differences and sometimes inherited pre-Islamic behaviour.

On the whole wherever Islam spread it purified the existing culture from past inhuman, unjust or unnatural habits and conditioning. Those customs that were found to be permissible, or indeed improved by Islam, were allowed to continue. While Islam suffused the old culture of the converts, producing an Islamic one in its stead, one must not fall into the simplistic fallacy that there was one Islamic culture, because Islam's dynamism transcends 'culture'. Its unifying force once translated into the arena of human life is ultimately neither social nor material but spiritual.

THE CULTURE OF MUSLIMS

> For every one of you we appointed a law and a way, and if Allah had pleased He would have made you a single people, but that He might try you in what He gave you. Therefore vie with one another in doing good. You will all return to Allah and He will inform you about that which you differed.
>
> Qur'an 5:48

The culture of Muslims has never been bound by geographical or climatic considerations, for Islam is a universal path and therefore accessible to all peoples. In 1990 it was estimated that there were over one billion Muslims living in disparate geographical areas covering several millions of square miles stretching all the way from China and the Pacific rim to the Atlantic, as well as in portions of Europe and more recently North America. Muslims have thus inhabited every possible climate and terrain. The Arabian heartland of Islam mainly encompassed the desert regions where scattered groups settled in oases, and nomadic pastoralists inhabited the vast but still habitable areas around the cities. Cultivated areas in the great river deltas where ancient cultures once flourished, such as the Nile Valley, Mesopotamia, the Indus valley and elsewhere, were farmed by peasant-folk.

The mountains, hills and forests found more towards the northern areas of Muslim lands were also home to many. Muslims are represented in every race, ranging from Chinese and Mongolian to Turkic, Aryan, Semitic, African, European and Indian.

The culture of any people is based upon sets of values and perceptions which motivate them to behave in a particular way, and there are several factors that underlie the distinctiveness of Muslim culture. It is primarily, of course, the *Din* and courtesy of Islam – the behavioral patterns, practices and perception of life – that have unified the Muslim peoples and which enable us to talk about an 'Islamic culture'. Because Muslims believe in the One All-embracing God and that this life is a preparation for the next, their perception, evaluation and living of life's experiences are shaped by the extent to which this understanding has been absorbed into their lives and transformed their outlook.

When different races, tribes and nations assimilate the *Din* deeply and correctly, one finds that they first identify themselves as Muslims before nations, societies or races. Equally, when Islam does not become deeply rooted in a people, the national, cultural or other group identities take precedence over their faith to the detriment of its application.

Although Islam naturally united the Muslim peoples, one cannot claim that it produced cultural uniformity. Everyday life in an Indian Muslim household in Delhi was not the same as that of its Moroccan counterpart in Marrakesh. However, they would have shared their love for the Prophet, their attitudes towards family honour (especially regarding their womenfolk) and towards their land, animals and shrines. Their religious festivals would be similar and they all aspired to go on *Hajj*. But the Indian family would also be very conscious of class or caste considerations and other related customs as an impinging legacy of Hinduism which would be alien to the Moroccan.

A second factor in uniting the Muslim masses was the inevitable use of Arabic. Because the Qur'an and traditions were in Arabic, Muslims naturally learnt it and that common denominator of language generated a basic sense of connection between them.

A third unifying factor underlying Muslim culture is the general uniformity of the religious rituals, especially the *Salat* and *Hajj*. The connective power of collectively performed, meaningful ritual is nowhere more epitomized than in the great universal and spiritual market-place of *Hajj*. The once-yearly pilgrimage brings truly diverse people together, placing them under the eye of God on a platform of equality in worldly status, humbled and dispossessed of any material or social power.

The unifying characteristics of Islam touch upon every aspect of life from the way a Muslim regards water (whether it is ritualistically pure to enable its use in ablution); to modesty regarding one's body (for both men and women); to protecting women from the harsher aspects of public life; to the etiquette of conducting fair and just business transactions; to upholding honourable conduct in war or peace. The entire spectrum of human experience is provided for in the *Din*.

FAMILY AND SOCIAL LIFE

O mankind, surely We have created you from a male and female and made you tribes and families that you may know each other. Surely the noblest of you with Allah is the most cautiously mindful [of his duty]. Surely Allah is Knowing, Aware.

Qur'an 49:13

Animals are programmed by nature to behave in a certain way. Limits to their behaviour are imposed upon them by natural phenomena, such as their physical strength, the ecological balance between their number and the availability of food and other factors that exert natural control.

In the case of human beings, however, there are in addition to many innately limiting factors other behavioural aspects that also have to be learned and adopted. These range from grooming the body to improving personal qualities. It is for this process of cultivation that Prophets and Messengers have arisen to help bridge that natural gap and give human beings the choice of completing their spiritual evolution. This process begins in a social arena, in the need for each other, for exchange and interaction. The foundation of that arena is the family and therefore the complementary relationship between man and woman.

The general nature of man is creative, expansive and destructive, whereas that of most women is more intuitive and nurturing, and therefore involved in the creational aspect of continuity. The complementarity of the two produces a natural harmony and equilibrium in existence, which is what we all seek. A woman seeks the reliability of manly energy while a man seeks the loyalty and availability of her womanly energy. Woman is beauty, man is majesty: when the two combine you have balance. Men can be brutally decisive and therefore wantonly destructive, while women tend to seek reconciliation and acceptability. When a man discovers the 'woman' within himself (that is, the qualities that predominate in and distinguish her gender), then he has reached a maturity that enables him to live harmoniously with any woman. The same principle applies to the woman.

Marriage and family life is a practice towards that ideal of fulfilment. This is why marriage is so highly recommended in Islam, for it allows the individual (man or woman) to rise into a higher inner state of complementarity and completion. Starting with the outer physical, the carnal even, moving towards balancing subtler needs and energies, marriage provides an arena for opposites to combine and contentment to be awakened within the individual.

There is a great deal in the Qur'an about the relationship between man and woman and about the practical details of marriage and divorce (which, though odious to a path that emphasizes unity, may in exceptional circumstances be necessary), particularly in chapters 2, 4, 24 and 33. The Prophet once said: 'The best of my people is he who shows his family perfect kindness and goodness.' There are numerous other traditions which speak against discord and harshness and which encourage goodwill and gentleness. The man's role as material provider and protector makes him responsible for the well-being of his household. Because of his responsibilities, he has been given the authority within his family so that its members can function fully and efficiently. His guardianship does not, however, preclude a woman from owning her own wealth. Indeed, the Prophet's wife Khadijah was extremely wealthy and chose to spend her wealth in the way of Allah.

Whether in rural villages or larger towns, Muslims have generally lived in multi-generational extended families which often included several cousins, aunts and uncles. These large households broke the isolation that can afflict the modern nuclear family. The pattern of responsibilities and social accountabilities of the extended family were very much based on Islamic norms, customs and values. Wherever the transformative vigour of Islam was diluted the very same structures of support often became causes for social stagnation.

Respect for elders, love and attention towards children, containment and co-operation rather than competitiveness are the norm for the Muslim family. In the interaction within and between such family units timeless and vitalizing qualities such as selflessness, generosity, patience and concern are reinforced.

In the best circumstances of Muslim life the woman has played a key role. In the present century this role has continued in rural areas, mostly out of necessity, but in urban situations her role has often been reduced to that of a domestic, lacking in education and social awareness, and therefore unable to contribute creatively to the wider spectrum of social life. This is not the position constantly emphasized by the Prophet and the Qur'an. If the liberation that Islam brings to all human beings is not allowed to be lived and fully applied, the oppressive aspects of tribalism and ignorance take over. The health of family life and the development it fuels in both the individual and society can only flourish if there is at its core an actively complementary partnership such as the Qur'an describes: 'They are an apparel for you and you are an apparel for them' (2:187).

THE CIVILIZING SCIENCES

The Prophet made it clear that seeking knowledge was obligatory for every Muslim, male or female. 'Seek knowledge even if it be in China', is a saying attributed to him, implying that one should go to great lengths in the pursuit of useful learning. Muslims did not have to go as far as that, however, before they discovered the philosophical, medical, aesthetic and other treasures of scholarship.

Possibly the greatest creative and rational act of the Muslims was their study and investigation of the knowledge developed in the classical Greek, Iranian, and Indian cultures, drawing from them what was useful and real through the 'filter' of Islamic understanding. The resulting hybrid of learning was the foundation for the far-reaching civilizing influence of the Muslims on world culture.

Scholarship and learning – literary, scientific, artistic, philosophical and spiritual – reached a peak period during the Abbasid caliphate of Al-Ma'mun (813–833), who established a major library in Baghdad called *Bayt al-Hikmah*, the 'House of Wisdom'. Later on the Fatimids established *Dar Al-'Ilm*, the 'House of Knowledge', in Cairo. These great repositories of books also housed centres for study, research and translation. In addition most mosques and *madrasahs* had libraries attached to them. By the mid-ninth century CE numerous libraries and centres of scholarship had been established in most large cities and towns. Painstakingly hand-copied books were also sold from bookshops that were frequently located near where the bazaars ended at the mosque.

The use of manufactured paper from the ninth century onwards made the copying of books cheaper and easier than the cruder papyrus and vellum of before. Through the Arabic language, beautifully hand-copied books spread this Muslim fusion of learning across the Muslim world and beyond into the Renaissance that led Europe out of the Dark Ages and into world domination.

Muslim historians traditionally began their study by first considering the history of the world and then focusing on the areas that most concerned them. Ibn Al-Athir (1163–1233) wrote the local history of Syria with that contextualizing approach, as did Al-Magrizi (d.1442) on Egypt. Al-Muqaddasi (d.1000) wrote a compendium of physical and classical geography of the known world based on eye-witness accounts and observations, while Al-Yaqt (d.1229) composed a geographical dictionary. Without doubt the greatest Muslim historian was Ibn Khaldun (d.1442), whose insight into human psychological and sociological functions created a framework of analysis and understanding that has singled him out as the 'Father' of historiography.

Astronomy had been developed from even earlier times for the purposes of calculating dates and time, and for navigation.

The Greek scientific tradition was combined with that of Iran and India which when rendered into Arabic ensured that it was preserved, developed and spread. In the health sciences the core of Muslim medical knowledge was taken from Galen, the great Greek anatomist and physician. It also developed from the work of Empedocles who in the fifth century put forward the view that the universe was composed of the four elements of fire, air, earth and water, and this conception developed into the doctrine that human health depended upon the harmonious balance of the four bodily humours.

The two greatest works on health during the Abbasid era were the *Haawi* (the 'Comprehensive' or 'All-containing') by the philosopher Abu Bakr Muhammad Al-Razi (863–925), also known as Rhazes and *Al-Qanun* (The Principles of Medicine) by the great philosopher Ibn Sina (Avicenna, 980–1037). Health sciences were propagated and transmitted through medical apprenticeship in the hospitals and clinics where the teaching took place. Numerous contributions to surgery and community health were also made, such as that of Ibn Al-Khatib (1313–1374), who was the first to understand the way plagues spread by contagion.

With regard to self-knowledge, which in modern times has been subsumed by 'psychology', a large body of knowledge was collected by the Sufis. Numerous interlinking models were developed with which to understand the self, how to treat and purify it and render the inner aspects of human life healthy and vital. This knowledge was mostly based on the Qur'an and the teachings of the Muslim saints and Sufi Shaykhs.

The Prophet indicated the way to gnosis when he said: 'Whoever knows himself knows his Lord.' Knowledge of the self was based on the premise that the individual self comes about when a spirit, whose nature it is not possible to comprehend, is brought about to activate and produce the individual soul in the womb. This soul (*nafs*) embarks upon a journey through this world towards the next, the purpose of this experience being to render the soul able to enter into the next world of non-time and non-space fully prepared. If it becomes attached and infatuated with this world, then it is doomed, which is one meaning of hell. But if it uses this world as an allegory for the essence that is behind it – which is permanent, ever-lasting and merciful – then the soul has been saved. The soul's purpose is to realize the Divine Essence behind the solid veil of physical existence. Every single person is endowed with the freedom to achieve that end through the life-transaction of submission based on trust and the sharpening of the innate, primal faculties of intuition and deeper understanding.

In the early period of Islam, Muslim writers took from the Greeks many aspects of dream interpretation. Dreams were considered an important part of an individual's life in the unseen, and Islamic literature on this subject is consequently very rich. Dreams were doors on to the world beyond the senses. The process of dreaming was explained thus: the soul, when released from the body during sleep, can perceive aspects of the subtler world. When it returns to the body it brings those perceptions with it and passes them on to the faculty of imagination (khayal) with appropriate images, which the sleeper then perceives as if by the senses.

Poetry and music also played a very important part in Arab and Islamic cultures. From before the Prophet's time, poetry had been the major artistic and creative outlet for the Arabs. Throughout the Arab Muslim world poetry was created in various forms, among which were the popular impromptu versions that were not written down, and rhyming prose was often employed as an aid to memory.

By the Umayyad times music had become a popular pastime for the ruling élite, despite disapproval by the legal orthodoxy. The king would often be concealed in court behind a curtain whilst musicians entertained him. The musical practices of the Abbasids were emulated in Spain and later on in the courts of the various other kingdoms and empires that emerged. The traditions that developed in the Andalusian courts were different, however, from those of the eastern Muslim lands, which were based on classical Iranian music. Singing was widely used on all sorts of occasions such as marriage, harvesting and warfare. Each region had its own tradition of song and musical instrumentation, which ranged from wind (flutes) to percussion and other basic devices. Some instruments, such as pipes and string instruments, were generally forbidden because they were traditionally associated with drunkards and therefore people of low moral character.

The Sufis also used a certain amount of music in their circles of *Dhikr* (remembrance) or *Sama'* (listening). Neither poetry nor music were considered forbidden in themselves. The *'Ulama* had defined the conditions in which performing and listening to music were permitted, namely that it should not be for frivolous amusement or to induce sensual or lustful agitation, and should certainly not be obscene or blasphemous. Imam Ghazali went so far as to say that through appropriate music the heart could be stirred into longing for God and thereby elevated on to a higher path.

MARKETS AND TOWNS

General patterns of urbanization in Muslim lands included market towns, garrisons that later grew into towns, and royal cities that grew around the ruler's palace and government buildings. Market towns were generally dominated by a local tribe and were thus under the authority of the tribal lord. Larger market towns tended to serve many of the smaller local ones. Seaside towns functioned as market towns in themselves as well as trading points. In most cities the merchants were a wealthy and important section of the population.

Like the breath from a living organism, food and raw materials flowed from the surrounding countryside and further afield into the towns and out again, onwards to other destinations. The volume and value of goods varied according to the storage capacity of each town as well as its proximity to trade routes. Some of the older Muslim cities, especially those surrounded by walls, have remained intact for several centuries, such as Khurasan in Iran, Aleppo in Syria, Fez in Morocco and Karbala in Iraq. Their bazaars and workshops remained in almost the same districts for centuries as the basic shape or centre of the city continued unaltered.

The bazaars were filled with goods pouring in along the

arteries of the trade routes. Raw materials came in, and finished goods were sent out. This natural pattern repeated itself in other aspects of urban life. For example, because of the Muslim sense of cleanliness and the need for ritually clean water, the supply of pure water was arranged to come in through a network of canals or cisterns at the higher end of a city, while the polluted water was expelled from the lower end. Tanneries and leather workshops were therefore often placed downwind close to where the waste-water flowed out.

A hierarchy of prestige in craftsmanship was reflected in the location of their shops within the bazaar, ranging from the jewellers and perfumeries at the top end, moving on through paper- and book-sellers, calligraphists, woodworkers, plaster workers and builders, until it ended with the tanners, dyers and butchers. On the periphery of the craftsmen's shops were the unskilled workers, the itinerant peddlers and street cleaners and other daily wage earners who would work on building sites, in gardens and other places in or around the city.

Most towns were surrounded by market gardens. The Prophet was known to have recommended against the building of large cities, so that every person could have easy access to the countryside and hear all the natural sounds of birds, animals, wind and water. On the outskirts of the cities were the caravanserais where long-distance trading caravans were rested and equipped, and where animals were bought. The floating population of the countryside flocked to these places to do their bidding and trading.

In all important cities there was a great affinity and interaction between the merchant families and master craftsmen, and the *Ulama* and jurists. Intermarriage between them stabilized the socio-economic structure of city life.

Conquered cities were modified in significant ways. For example, the large congregational Friday mosque would be located as centrally as possible. The *souk* or bazaar would also be reorganized in greater accordance with Muslim sensibilities, so that the parts more often frequented by women (such as the fabric stalls) were more accessible to them.

Cities often housed distinctive ethnic or tribal quarters, sometimes according to professions and trades. Each quarter had its own mosque, or, if it was Jewish or Christian, a

Synagogue or Church. Public bath houses also abounded and were well frequented.

In cities designed and built by Muslims the mosque would lie in the heart of the city. In Cairo the Al-Azhar mosque was built by the Fatimids for the teaching and dissemination of Islam on a grand scale. Many Muslim cities often had at their centre the shrine of a saint or great Muslim leader, such as the tomb of Mulay Idris which stands near to the great teaching mosque of Qarawiyyin at the centre of Fez.

Thus the locus of worship, whether a great mosque or shrine, became the point from which the culture and economic life of the city radiated. Political power, however, lay elsewhere, namely with the royal court. Isolation of the ruler from the ruled became with time an increasing necessity until the Abbasids actually moved up the river Tigris from Baghdad to build Samarra. From that time separation became the practised rule which was followed by many other subsequent rulers. Their seclusion was initially an expression of their power and magnificence, and it also kept their soldiers removed from contact with urban interests, which could perhaps arouse unwanted reactions. The degree of their enforced distance varied from dynasty to dynasty and from age to age. The Mamluk rulers of Egypt, for example, were very secluded, whereas the Hafsids of Tunis were less so, and the early Safavids were yet more accessible.

By the fifteenth century, in the commercial sections of the souk or city one would often find a large building constructed around a courtyard with storerooms on the ground floor and above them the equivalent of a hotel. These inns or city caravanserais were called a Khan, Funduq or Qaysariyyah. Certain Khans specialized in food stuffs, others in carpets, and yet others in manufactured goods.

Family houses were similarly built in two to three storeys around courtyards with small internal gardens. All the rooms of the house would have looked out on to these gardens. The size and height of the rooms, and other architectural features, differed slightly from one region to another, moulded by geographical position and the indigenous crafts. Windows and wooden screens were commonly used, especially in the warmer climates, to let in the breeze and afford some privacy.

Many of the older houses in Granada or Seville still maintain this style that had existed from India to Morocco.

TRADE AND FINANCE

Allah has allowed trade and forbidden usury.

Qur'an 2:275

And whatever you lay out as usury so that it may increase in the property of men, it increases not with Allah.

Qur'an 30:39

In a short ninth-century treatise on trade in Iraq we are given the following information: From the Kazars came slaves, armour, helmets and hoods. From India came tigers, leopards, elephants, deerskins, rubies, sandalwood, ebony and coconut. From China aromatics, silk, porcelain, paper, ink, peacocks, wild horses, saddles, felt and cinnamon. From Byzantium silver and gold vessels, imperial Dinars, embroidered cloth, brocade, red copper, locks, water engineers, marble workers and eunuchs. No doubt imports from Europe were too insignificant at the time to be mentioned but by the Middle Ages European weaponry and English wool had also begun to be imported into the Muslim world.

From early on non-Muslims were granted safe conduct to visit Muslim lands for commerce and trade. Their commercial activities resulted in a growing number of non-Muslim resident communities of traders, some of whom were European. By Ottoman times trade in weapons from Europe and the Muslim world had grown considerably. By the sixteenth century there was strong competition between European merchants and governments to supply war materials to the Turks, and by the late eighteenth century the balance of trade had changed decisively in favour of Europe. The rapid growth of European industry greatly increased this unequal flow of trade. The establishment of colonies in the New World as well as the commercial outposts in the East subsequently gave the European merchants an advantageous dimension to their trade with their Middle Eastern customers.

From the beginning of the eighteenth century, whilst Europe

THE ELEMENTS OF ISLAM

had once imported numerous products from the Muslim Middle East, it was now mostly importing raw material and exporting manufactured goods, such as cloth, implements and weapons. Until then products like coffee, tea and sugar had constituted the major exports from the Middle East, but by the middle of the eighteenth century the Dutch were growing coffee in Java, and the French were exporting coffee grown in the West Indies to Turkey, which by 1739 was cheaper than the coffee coming from Ethiopia and southern Arabia. Sugar used to be exported from India and Iran but by 1671 the French were processing cane from their West Indian colonies in their refineries in Marseilles and selling it east at cheaper prices than local sugar. Tobacco, of course, was mostly the preserve of European, British and American trade because it was brought in from the Americas.

By the end of the eighteenth century the feeble and weakened economies of Muslim lands contrasted very strongly with the vigorous trade, commerce and industry of Europe. The Jewish minority played a significant role in every trade, ranging from manufactured goods to raw materials and foods such as wheat. It was during the nineteenth century that European economic, monetaristic and industrial supremacy became clearly dominant, so that all the Muslim rulers of Turkey, Egypt, Iran and elsewhere were competing with each other to obtain Western products and loans, and seeking to transplant Western practices and industry in the hope of rapidly transforming their societies.

The etiquette and rules of commercial transaction were developed according to Islamic values. This was evident to a very great degree in the Andalusian towns and Ottoman territories where prefects and monitors maintained these standards through the agency of a *Muhtasib* or *Muqaddir* (value appraiser). Most Muslim trading establishments did not, however, develop extensive administrative networks for the volume of trade remained on a small scale.

Islam forbids usury and all situations where interest is fixed. However, in many cities Jews and other minorities did practise usury and money-lending. In India, for example, Hindu moneylenders ended up owning huge portions of towns and entire villages when Muslim debtors defaulted on their loans. Through neglect compounded by a usurious European financial system already in place (having been developed for over four hundred years), Muslims ignored the development of a system which could cope with the increasing complexity of world trade and finance. Rulers preferred to leave such matters in foreign hands, such as the Jews and later the Americans, because they were not beholden to act Islamically, and a foreign non-Muslim under royal protection would not expose a ruler to his people for his un-Islamic conduct because they had too much to gain.

Many Muslim rulers loved to dazzle their populace with exclusive, imported technologies. Their agents were primarily Christians, Jews, Armenians and Hindus. At one point the Moroccan treasury was in the hands of an English dentist while one eighth of the treasury went to pay for his hobby of photography. In Persia incredible amounts were spent on fireworks. The rulers of Oudh in Lucknow imported British gentlemen to teach them how to set up banquets, and as far back as 250 years ago they were the largest importers of cut crystal from Europe which they used to impress local British rulers. There were no real Muslims in seats of power; had they been they would have had to develop and maintain a financial system that was not based on usury and the inevitable exploitation of illusory money.

RULERS AND THE RULED

Islam assumes that the governing élite should be an example upholding the highest level of Islamic ethical conduct, both in their outer rituals as well as in their personal qualities. When, however, this is not realized a clear division appears between the class of rulers and the ruled. Such divergence in the history of Muslims has often led to confrontation and revolt.

An institutionalized separation between the rulers and the ruled had begun from the death of the fourth Caliph 'Ali, when the objectives and lifestyle of the Umayyad Caliphs and courtiers diverged from the general Muslim public. This state of affairs continued almost throughout the entire history of Muslims. In the early days it was Byzantine and Persian Sassanian administrators and court advisors who helped

133

Muslim rulers in fiscal and other bureaucratic controls. These were gradually replaced by other non-Muslims and foreigners who not only dealt with matters of finance but also military affairs and foreign relations.

The *Ulama* of the courts were all highly domesticated, often chosen for their tolerance, support and ability to rationalize the rulers' decisions and actions according to Islamic legal and theological precept. These *Ulama* were often held in contempt by ordinary people, echoing what the Prophet had said, 'I fear for my people [on account of] the *Ulama* who condone the rulers.'

For the most part court life and public life continued in parallel giving rise to a culture of accord and mutual understanding. As long as the ruler appeared to be reasonably just and not too oppressive, the two tiers co-existed. Occasionally, however, confrontations erupted and in most cases the rulers resorted to brutality and sheer force, manipulation and certain compromising adjustments.

Because the Shi'i maintained that the right to rule Muslims belongs to the qualified Imam, in whose absence only the most pious and knowledgeable could rule, the majority of the Shi'is either opposed or ignored the institution of kings and sultans. The Sunnis on the other hand often accepted the rule of any Muslim as long as he professed Islam and the majority of the populace acquiesced.

The general population had their own hierarchy of *Ulama* as well as of leaders of commerce, artisans and landowners. The 'people's' system was allowed to function as long as the ruler was paid his taxes and allowed to requisition his recruits. These *Ulama* and mosques maintained their independence from ruling interests through endowments, often in the form of shops and other sources of income.

This was the general arrangement until the emergence of the twentieth-century modern Muslim 'state', the model for which was imported from the West and forcibly grafted on to Muslim lands, for it was not an indigenously cultivated model. From then on all mosques and other Muslim institutions were absorbed by the governments, thus coming directly under centralized rule. By the middle of the twentieth century, the new-style governments controlled every aspect of the life of the Muslim masses. This resulted in the rise of numerous opposition groups, frequent confrontation and all kinds of social upheaval and disasters. In the past the alienation of the rulers from the ruled had seldom resulted in such major clashes because people had been left alone to live their 'separate' lives.

The situation in contemporary 'Muslim states' is such that the rulers' version of Islam is often no more than a ritualistic veneer, bearing no resemblance to the divine prophetic model. Pious and serious Muslims often consider their governments as traitors to the true cause of Islam, and all attempts to democratize or parliamentize their method of government have therefore resulted in failure or are a mere cosmetic face-lift to ensure Western approval.

SPECIAL ISSUES IN MUSLIM LIFE

JEWS, CHRISTIANS AND OTHERS LIVING AMONG MUSLIMS

The Islamic attitude towards religious minorities allowed them to function according to their norms and customs and to be judged according to their own systems of religious law, as long as they did not interfere publicly with the Muslim practices or engage in activities that were un-Islamic. However, by the twentieth century this latter condition had been considerably relaxed. Most of the trade in wine and spirits and, indeed, the actual manufacture of alcoholic beverages and other commodities forbidden in Islam, as well as usurious money-lending, was in the hands of Jews or Christians who accumulated great wealth by doing so.

Jews were widely spread throughout the Muslim world. Living mostly in cities or smaller towns, their occupations were chiefly in trade, crafts and other commercial activities. In the Maghreb a sizeable part of the peasantry had been converted to Judaism before the coming of Islam, and some rural Jewish communities existed in the Yemen and the Fertile Crescent.

The majority of the Jews in the Middle East belonged to the tradition of oral law and interpretation of the Talmud and were trained in Talmudic scholarship. A large portion of the

Jewish communities were Arabic speaking, but used Hebrew for liturgical purposes. Iraq had been the main centre of Arab Jewry, from where they had exercised considerable influence until the formation of Israel, when they were forcibly induced to emigrate there.

Christianity in North Africa, especially in the Maghreb, had dwindled and virtually disappeared by the twelfth century. The Coptic Church, however, remained a very important element in Egypt, although the number of Copts was not growing, and in some areas was actually shrinking. Throughout Syria and northern Iraq Christian communities remained in a diminished form. In cities the majority of Christians belonged to the Eastern Orthodox Church, but there were also the Syrian Orthodox or Nestorians. In Lebanon and parts of Syria there was a fourth church, the Maronite, which had accepted the Roman Catholic doctrine when the Crusaders had invaded the coast.

When the early Muslims conquered existing cities the inhabitants belonged to the Jewish, Christian or other religious communities. Forcible conversion was very rare and on many occasions Muslim rulers preferred the Jews and Christians to retain their religion for the various reasons already outlined. They had to pay a poll tax and obey certain rules, such as not wearing green (the traditional colour associated with Islam) and not carrying arms when on horseback. These restrictions were not, however, uniformly enforced. A Muslim man could marry a Jewish or Christian woman, but a non-Muslim man could not marry a Muslim woman unless he converted to Islam. Nor could a non-Muslim inherit from a Muslim.

It was not only in the fields of trade, finance and the administration of Muslim societies that the Jews, Christians and especially the Copts were very important elements. For long periods of time in many Muslim cities Jews had practised medicine, and many famous court doctors were either Jewish or Christian. A large number of them converted to Islam, which further elevated their status, and as a result they enjoyed great power over the ruling élite. High-value craftsmanship and trade in gold and silver, as well as in medicines was in the hands of Jews and Christians, often working for themselves and sometimes in collaboration with Muslims.

The Christian and Jewish communities were bound together by the solidarity of their local grouping clustered around their Church or Synagogue, as well as by their higher authorities. The Patriarchs and Bishops of the Christians, such as the Nestorian Patriarch in Baghdad during the Abbasid rule, or the Coptic Patriarch in Cairo, held special positions of influence and respect. These religious minorities often had a special representative with a strong direct connection with the court, and they enjoyed better representation and protection than that given to local Muslims. For example, it was more likely for a Jewish merchant who had been robbed outside the city to receive quicker and more effective support from the authorities than might be the case for a local Muslim merchant.

MODEST DRESS AND *HIJAB*

The injunction for women to dress modestly has become a stumbling block much focused on in the popular media, whereas it is in fact very natural for a woman to be modest and for men to respect that modesty. The Qur'an says:

> O children of Adam! We have indeed sent down to you clothing to cover your shame and [clothing] for beauty and clothing guards [against evil]; that is the best. This is of the messages of Allah that they may be mindful.
>
> (7:26)

All Muslims, men and women alike, must cover themselves and avoid revealing clothes which are designed to accentuate and enhance the contours of the body and emphasize its physical beauty.

The Qur'an is very clear on the matter:

> Say to the believing men that they lower their gaze and restrain their sexual passions. That is purer for them. Surely Allah is Aware of what they do. And say to the believing women that they lower their gaze and restrain their sexual passions and do not display their adornment except what appears thereof, and let them wear their head-covering over their bosoms. And they should not display their adornment except to their husbands or fathers or the fathers of their husbands or their sons . . .
>
> (24:30–31)

The prophetic teachings do not prescribe any particular style or type of dress. We are only given a broad description of what is acceptable and what is prohibited. The Prophet clarified that the attractive parts of the anatomy should be covered except the face, hands and feet. Neither the Qur'an nor the Prophet ordered tent-like clothing, *burqas* or the like. These oppressive costumes were a cultural and ethnic invention.

Muslims are discouraged from being excessively concerned with personal beauty, yet it is permitted to have as fine and varied a wardrobe as one likes, if it is within one's means. Gold and silk are luxuries reserved exclusively for women, for Islam prohibits men from wearing silk clothes and gold jewellery. Rings are not forbidden to them but they should be made of silver.

The word *hijab* in Arabic means a barrier, cover or veil, and its main purpose is to reduce potential agitation, desire and attraction between men and women who are not partners or not intending to be partners. Inner *hijab* relates to modesty, lowering of the eyes and being conscious not to arouse the interest of the opposite sex. When inner *hijab* is accompanied by outer 'announced' *hijab* then the purpose is complete.

MULTIPLE MARRIAGE

Marriage is regarded as a sacred bond reinforced by mutual love, tender feeling and collaboration between man and woman. With time and correct attention the relationship between partners will grow in depth and magnitude. Marital union is usually further bonded by the birth of children.

Multiple marriage was prevalent among all nations of antiquity, but without limits or conditions. Before the advent of Muhammad, the world in general and Arabia in particular treated women unjustly and with depravity. The historic facts give us many horrific pictures which are set among all echelons of all societies, East and West.

Islam permits a restricted type of multiple marriage, but does not always encourage it. A man can under no circumstance marry more than four wives at a time, and then only if he is sure that he can do justice to all four in all aspects of life as laid down by the Qur'an and the prophetic teachings. If he has the slightest doubt about being just, then the Qur'an tells him: 'If you fear that you will not do justice then [marry] only one wife' (4:3).

DIVORCE

Separation and the break-up of a union is an undesirable experience for all involved. When a man and woman have embarked on a marriage they must endeavour to do their utmost to maintain and deepen that relationship. Even when differences appear and circumstances become difficult, Muslims are exhorted to seek help through the intervention of intermediaries and wise counsel. The Qur'an and the Prophet strongly recommend reconciliation and forgiveness. The Prophet warned: 'Among all permissible things divorce is the most hateful to God.'

Divorce is the last resort. If, however, reconciliation is not possible, or there are other factors that mitigate divorce (such as insanity), then divorce can be resorted to providing certain conditions are observed.

SLAVES

Slavery in Muslim society originates from the time when Muslims were at war with pagan or primitive peoples. Whoever was captured and spared death was given the chance to discover Islam as the path to knowledge of the Creator. Among the charitable acts of the early community in Medina was the purchase of slaves so as to teach them the *Din* and eventually set them free. However, like other Islamic practices, this pattern changed considerably to suit the purposes of ignorant people, and in some cases became grounds for abuse.

The idea of slavery did not have the same association for Muslim societies as it did in the countries of North and South America. Slavery under Europeans was based on the total subjugation of slaves without any possibility for change in their status. In Islamic law a slave was given a recognized position. According to that law, a free-born Muslim could not be enslaved, and non-Muslim slaves captured in war or procured by other ways (such as children born of slaves) were to be treated with justice and kindness. It was also considered a highly meritorious act to free them. As a result of these legal provisions the relationship between master and slave was a close one and often continued even after the slave was freed. In many cases a freed slave might marry the master's daughter and conduct his business for him. Numerous Muslim rulers and leaders married women slaves, and many kings and sultans were the product of such wedlock (the Caliph Al-Ma'mun was one). Many of the Shi'i Imams, saints and outstanding Muslim scholars were the sons of slaves.

During Abbasid rule another category of slaves appeared – that of military slaves. These were brought in from central Asia and kept for the sole purpose of protecting the ruler. The Mamluks, who ruled Egypt and Syria from 1250–1517, were soldiers who had been recruited for this purpose, but converted to Islam and were subsequently freed.

In Muslim cities slaves were for the most part domestic servants and concubines. They were also used as eunuchs to guard the women of the noble élite and the more secluded parts of the household. It was quite a common feature in Muslim society to allow a slave to occupy a position of great influence and power, and to be called a slave was not derogatory.

Many Europeans, and Christian and Jewish merchants in the port cities of Italy, France and Greece were engaged in the export of slaves to the Muslim world. During the eighth century the Venetians competed with the Greeks for this trade and were known to have been the main suppliers of eunuchs both to the Byzantine courts and Muslim kingdoms. The trafficking of slaves between Europe and the Muslim world continued from the Middle Ages up until the fifteenth century when the Muslims gained direct access to sources themselves in the Slavic lands. The Ottoman wars in Europe brought large numbers of Christian slaves including Albanians Slavs. Except for isolated instances, the slave trade had died out by the twentieth century.

PRESENT-DAY MUSLIMS

The general conditions of life for Muslims in the second half of the twentieth century can only be understood if we consider the totality of all the factors shaping their current situation. One of the most important points is the present geo-political distribution of Muslims. The majority of Muslims live in so-called Muslim states, many of which are Arabic speaking (nearly one-sixth of all Muslims are Arabs) joined together by a powerless political coalition called the Arab League (established in 1945). In 1971 over forty governments with Islam as their declared state religion joined together in an Organization of the Islamic Conference, and by 1992 there were forty-six members of the OIC.

The reality is that Muslim states are continuously embroiled in senseless controversy and even political or military confrontation with each other. There is very little real harmony between them or a common higher objective. Muslims within these states are also divided in a broader sense along ethnic, racial, sectarian and linguistic lines. Sectarianism within the Sunni majority as well as between Sunnis and Shi'is is often exploited. The unifying attributes of Islam – humanity, reasonableness, piety, submission to Allah, knowledge of the Qur'an and way of the Prophet of Allah – are not the primary objectives of Muslim rulers or their state policies. Present-day Muslims are divided by artificial geo-political lines and ruled by puppet kings, sultans and presidents who are allied to or nominated by Western diktat, upon whose advice, technology and economic control they are dependent.

Within these states much official propaganda and discussion about the glory of past Islam is indulged in. Thus we see and hear of Islamic conferences, Islamic parties, Islamic banks and even enforced Islamic codes. As the Islamic sentiment of the masses grows their governments label most of their acts as 'Islamic', without any true spiritual conviction or transformation.

For the first time this century, however, the shock of the Islamic revolution in Iran brought the decaying conditions of Muslims sharply into focus and triggered off attempts to arrest this decay and possibly renew and revive the *Din* of

Islam. The rise of Islam in Iran, and its challenge to the techno-imperial power of America, resulted in a decade of war against Iran, fought of course by proxy of the brutal Iraqi government with aid and encouragement from Arab Muslim states under the supervision of the West. The events in Iran brought about widespread interest and debates throughout the Muslim world.

The superficial divisions among Muslims are perpetuated by the lack of proper basic education. This lack is comprehensive for it includes the Qur'anic and prophetic teachings, in particular the higher spiritual values of the *Din*. The historical neglect of the education of Muslim women has ensured that the mother is left ignorant and thus bound to raise children in an un-Islamic manner. The Prophet said: 'The true school is the mother,' a tradition which, like many others, is often repeated and little acted upon. The Prophet also called upon Muslims to seek knowledge 'even if it was in China' (i.e. far away) but, as we have seen, the Qur'anic and spiritual knowledge of Islam have become the preserve of a few specialists while the majority of Muslims remain content with outer Islamic cultural or ethnic trappings.

A contributing factor to the lack of Muslim mass education is the dominance of a class of professional *'Ulama* and *Mullas* – the so-called 'clergy'. As they established themselves as the guardians of the *Din*, people complacently delegated their religious duties to this class of experts instead of fulfilling the prophetic injunction for everyone – man and woman alike – to strive to gain full spiritual knowledge. And so we now have the dismal but common scenario of Muslims paying someone else to recite the Qu'ran once in a while, usually on the occasion of a bereavement, instead of learning and acting upon the Qur'an itself.

Islam teaches that it is the community that has to perform all functions of the life-transaction for themselves and by themselves, and not to rely on specialist professionals. In fact, it is a blameworthy act to be paid for teaching religion, reading the Qur'an or even being an undertaker. The community is beholden to serve itself and thereby increase human interaction and interdependence.

The slow erosion of Islamic values and way of life during this century, coupled with Western material, monetary, technological, educational, and political dominance over Muslim lands, has caused most Muslims to imitate Western culture wholesale as an act of 'progress'. Blind westernization has naturally resulted in frustration, disappointment, anger and nostalgia, and sometimes a desperate desire to revive the Din at any cost. The average educated Muslim continues to be confused about the possibility of modernization without de-spiritualizing westernization. A natural outcome of this confusion is seen in frequent upheavals, usually accompanied by ineffective anti-Western slogans, and various other forms of emotional and sometimes violent defiance, ranging from small demonstrations to hostage-taking and major revolutions. Many Muslims feel nostalgic for the past, disappointed in the present, angry with unjust rulers, and despairing as a result of poverty, exploitation, and other inhuman and un-Islamic conditions.

Large numbers of Muslims also live in non-Muslim states throughout the world. For example, the population of Muslims in India, which is secular, is greater than that in Muslim Pakistan. Most Muslims living in the West are economic emigrants from Asia or Africa, with the exception of a small but increasing number of converts. Although these immigrants have brought with them some of their national, ethnic ways and customs peculiar to their individual cultural backgrounds, their descendants are gradually rediscovering original Islam and its high values and moral standards, as their inherited cultural baggage is gradually peeled off.

Younger Muslim generations in the West are no longer hypnotized by the myth of an alternative system for honourable and fulfilling human interaction other than the sublime path of Islam. In a shrinking world where it is becoming increasingly clear that the emperor has no clothes, their awakening is gradually being shared throughout the Muslim world. The myth and collapse of Communism can only be followed by the discovery of the falsehood of apparently civilized Capitalism. The idol of Capitalism is being dethroned.

THE FUTURE OF ISLAM

> ... Allah never changes a favour [condition] which He has conferred upon a people until they change what is in their own selves, and surely Allah is Hearing, Knowing.
>
> Qur'an 8:53

The Muslim world, and indeed the rest of the world, has been overcome by the commercial, technological, monetaristic and political dominance of the West. More than a thousand million Muslims are divided into hundreds of economically impoverished, politically and socially divided groups. Whenever a people forget that the purpose of this life is to know the Lifegiver, they become denuded of any creative energy or vitality, spiritual or material.

The rest of the world is also undergoing a similar process of fragmentation and erosion of moral and higher human values. The early power and oppressive dominance of the Church with its superstitious dogmas were finally rendered ineffectual by the scientific and Industrial Revolution, which reduced its power to mere ceremony. Real power went into manufacturing, production, finance and commerce. Until that time, however, commerce had been subservient or married to the Church. Whenever commerce superseded the authority of the Church it was broken, as in the case of the Knights Templar, who were in effect the first European banking system.

By the nineteenth century the power of money and banking had overtaken every other power base. The advent of sophisticated industry, vast supra-national commercial concerns, and the two World Wars of the twentieth century have globalized the power of money. With the crumbling of Communism the cantilever equilibrium of Capitalism has disappeared, and there is no clear political direction for the so-called world leaders. The Church lies defunct, the creative manufacturing period is effectively over, and the hopes aroused by the promise of science and money together solving the human problem have been shattered. In the post Gulf War era, the fragments of atomization of the human situation are evident everywhere. This is the day of reckoning, the day of which the Qur'an says: 'Whither to flee?' (75:10). This is precisely

144

the point where a grassroots awakening to original Islam is most likely, initially on an individual basis, and leading later to collective and societal communities.

In the present world situation there are several factors that will influence the future course of Islam. With the coming of the jet age and satellite communication, the world has indeed become a closely interlinked global entity. The egalitarian advantages of independent civil and municipal services are universally acknowledged. The military is no longer of any consequence as it is subservient to the monetary system. The ultimate decision for the deployment of military force in the West is based on economic factors.

Muslims in the East are beginning to realize the extent of the erosion of both their material and moral inheritance. The rapid rate of population growth in many Muslim countries compounded by increasing literacy and higher education is bound to produce greater awareness and deeper natural connections between Muslims in all parts of the world, in spite of state controls and political barriers.

It is unlikely that Muslim countries will go through the same rational and evolutionary processes of economic union that have taken place in Europe. People themselves will begin to find that they have much in common with other Muslims across the border because Islam does not differentiate between race or colour. They will begin to discover the collective strength which they had lost, and will rediscover their true *Din*. Artificial state borders will be ignored and in time disappear in the same way that the Soviet Union has disintegrated. As the so-called 'Muslim states' become ineffective and redundant, a new system will arise which will be totally different from anything we have experienced to date. It will not be based on a Western-style federation or union, themselves the sophisticated products of a long history of economic rationalization; for while Muslims may have adopted a Western-style civil service and the ideals of democracy, they have no concomitant technological or monetaristic tradition to support these structures. What is more likely to happen is a spontaneous and organic rise of coalitions between people, but not based on a centrally governed state. 'Self-regulating anarchy' may well be the most appropriate description of the early stages of the new order.

Islam will not rise universally in any shape that we can predict because it has never before occurred on a global scale. The world is now so interlinked, however, that Islam will make its impact in a manner which no one can reliably forecast.

An important factor is the growing number of Muslims in the Western world, which is estimated at over 20 million if we include North America. Whilst this number is steadily increasing (Islam is the fastest growing religion in the world), awareness of Islamic teachings as well as commitment to the Din is growing in parallel.

Arab nationalism and statism are ideas from the past. In the meantime, Islam has broken loose from the past barriers of tribal or cultural confinements. The original prophetic teachings are as clear and timeless as ever. Original Islam will be rediscovered once people become tired of looking for salvation in the godless post-economic deserts. For the intelligent, sincere seeker there is no excuse or escape from the prophetic way.

The future of Islam will start, not with some evangelical event, but by simple transformation through suffering and destitution. It will begin with love for true Islam in the hearts of men and women, from which will rise the post-modern Islamic way of life, bubbling out beyond and above state boundaries, selfish regulations, and all other artificial barriers.

Islam recognizes only one barrier, and that is ignorance of Allah, for it leads to living in this world without a spiritual ideal and framework of moral conduct. To live truly in Islam is to be accountable to Allah at all times, remembering death with every breath, and it is from that remembrance that every instant of life becomes a living experience. The awakened Muslim interacts in this world as a courteous wayfarer, taking what is essential to continue on the journey of discovery. The path begins by acknowledging the outer creational world, and leads to the discovery of the ever-present Divine Light within. When this mature state is achieved, then the original human virtues of love, generosity, tolerance and service to others become the order of the day and the foundation for a moral and just society.

EPILOGUE

Surely there is a reminder in this for him who has a heart or he gives ear and is a witness.

Qur'an 50:37

Islam is the last divine reminder to mankind of the human potential, duty and way to re-create the original garden in our hearts and on earth. This can only happen if we are trained and educated in self-knowledge. With that comes acceptance and submission to the Glorious Creator who created out of love in order to be known, worshipped and adored:

'I was a hidden treasure and I loved to be known, therefore I created.'

(*Sacred Tradition*)

Man's search for biological or creational roots is only a prelude to, or a reflection of, the search for his spiritual origins, which is what the path of Islam will lead him to. The present-day global convergence gives us greater hope in developing clearer understanding and realizing justice, peace and harmony for humankind. Although there appear to be ethnic, religious, national or material differences between people, the real differences are based on techno-economic iniquities that result in exploitative monopolies (generally held by supra-national corporations). However, the collapse of Communism and the end of global political polarization could become the ashes out of which a more equitable world rises, if we awaken to the higher elements within ourselves and work towards living those greater virtues.

A purely structuralist, materialist approach to existence, be it in the field of science, sociology or psychology, has failed. This failure has taken us to the point where we can re-emerge through the discovery of the transformative path of Islam. In order for us to improve the human situation we need not only to use our rational capacities but also to purify our hearts. Thus will the vistas of inspiration and creative interaction expand. The basic highway code of Islamic conduct – trust in Allah, love of the Prophet that manifests in his emulation, submission, outer service and inner joy – makes this possible in the smoothest way. Once the process of transformation and inner fulfilment has begun, its effect will snowball until a time when there will be enough people with this enlightened outlook to sufficiently influence a natural re-emergence of the divine qualities in humanity. This transformation alone will re-awaken hearts and souls and direct them with clarity, joy and honour towards their Creator to whom they are already journeying, inexorably, since the day they were born.

APPENDIX :
OUTSTANDING MUSLIMS

The Qur'an describes those who are most honoured by Allah among men and women as those who are the most pious in remembrance of Allah. The great Muslims mastered combinations of numerous disciplines and knowledges and were acknowledged as outstanding by their peers and other leading Muslims.

Because so many of them were polymaths it is difficult to categorize them according to the skill or subjects for which they subsequently became known. For example At-Tabari, a ninth/tenth-century scholar from northern Iran whose work on history earned him renown, was also a great commentator on the Qur'an and an acknowledged expert on other sciences. The objective of the serious or scholarly Muslim was not to specialize in one field of academic study, but to gain knowledge of God and His creation. We therefore find that the gamut of natural sciences, history and above all the religious sciences were all explored as part of the final quest: knowledge of Allah.

It is a historically significant fact that most of these outstanding Muslims were not Arabs, though they were all masters of the Arabic language and often lived in the Arab lands of the Muslim world.

The list of outstanding Muslim women would be extensive

had it not been for the fact that very little has been written about them in publicly available records and literature. This lack of recording is due to the general tradition of women's natural self-effacement, and their being the 'hidden' teachers and saints without feeling compelled to announce themselves. For example the great Shaykh Ibn 'Arabi gained his first foundations in *tasawwuf* from two women saints.

By no means exhaustive, the following list (chronologically arranged according to dates of death) is a small selection of some of the most famous Muslim personalities and leaders whose names have also become familiar in the West, and whose influence on the development of human knowledge has been long-lasting.

ZAYNAB BINT 'ALI (c.684) was the Prophet's granddaughter and a truly heroic example of womanly virtue and honour. This was revealed when, after the martyrdom of her beloved brother Imam Husayn at Karbala, she was taken prisoner along with the other remaining women and children of their party, and confronted the tyranny and injustice of the Umayyad rulers.

HASAN AL-BASRI (d.728) was considered to be the earliest Sufi. Born in Medina, the son of a freed slave, he later settled in Basrah, Iraq. Many Sufi *tariqahs* claim connection to him and through him to Imam 'Ali and the Prophet.

JA'FAR AS-SADIQ (d.765) was a descendant of the Prophet, and a renowned scholar of religious and natural sciences. Malik Ibn Anas and Abu Hanifa were among his students estimated at over four thousand. The Shi'is consider him to be the founder of their School of Law, called *Ja'fari Fiqh*.

ABU HANIFA (d.767) was the founder of the Hanafi School of Law that is dominant in India, Pakistan and the Middle East. He was born in Kufah of Persian origin and died imprisoned in Baghdad because of his support for a Zaydi revolt.

MALIK IBN ANAS (d.795), the founder of the Maliki School of Law, was born and died in Medina. His book, *Al-Muwatta*, is the earliest collection of *Hadith*, and his first book of law. *Maliki fiqh* is dominant in North and West Africa.

RABI'AH AL-'ADAWIYYAH (d.801) was one of the most famous women saints in Islam. She extolled the way of divine love and intimacy with God. A contemporary of Hasan al-Basri, her life in Basrah was marked by extreme asceticism.

NAFISAH (c.830) was a great granddaughter of 'Ali Ibn Abi Talib. Born in Mecca, she later migrated with her husband to Egypt to escape persecution. Most of her life was spent fasting and in night vigils of prayer. While still alive she had her grave dug and recited the Qur'an several thousand times while sitting in it. People still throng to her tomb in today's Cairo.

AHMAD IBN HANBAL (d.855) founded the Hanbali School of Law which grew out of his selection of *Hadith* entitled *Al-Masnad*. *Hanbali fiqh* prevails in Saudia Arabia and other Gulf states.

ABU YUSUF YA'QUB IBN AL-KINDI (d.870) was the first important philosopher in Islam and a master of calligraphy, mathematics, chemistry, astronomy and medicine. Al-Kindi's philosophical approach was based on harmony between reason and revelation and he advocated allegorical interpretation of the Qur'an.

ABU 'ISA MUHAMMAD AT-TIRMIDHI (d.892), a blind scholar possibly from the area around Balkh, travelled extensively to gather *Hadith* which he collected into what became one of the six canonical collections.

HUSAYN IBN MANSUR AL-HALLAJ (d.922) was a famous Persian mystic accused of heresy and executed by the establishment because of his frequent shocking outbursts expressing his inner intoxications and union with God.

ABU JA' FAR MUHAMMAD IBN AT-TABARI (d.923), a scholar from northern Iran, was a prolific writer on theology, literature and history.

ABU BAKR MUHAMMAD IBN ZAKARIYYA AR-RAZI (d.925) came to be known as Rhazes in the West as his teachings were followed by Nicholas Flamel, Paracelsus, and others. A Persian physician, he wrote on various topics in medicine including the role that psychosomatic medicine, or self-suggestion, plays in healing.

ABU'L HASAN 'ALI IBN ISMA'IL AL-ASH'ARI (d.935), born and raised in Basrah, was a great authority on dialectical theology, counteracting the Mu'tazilis, whose work created a basis for Sunni dogma.

ABU NASR MUHAMMAD AL-FARABI (d.950) was born in Turkestan, studied in Baghdad and died in Damascus. A great philosopher who integrated Platonic and Aristotelian thought, which was later adopted by Saint Thomas Aquinas. Included among his many original works were those on music and mathematics.

ABU'L HASAN 'ALI IBN AL-HUSAYN 'ALI AL-MAS'UDI (d.956), a historian, geographer, philosopher and natural scientist. He was born in Baghdad and studied under the best teachers of his day.

MUHAMMAD IBN ISHAQ IBN AN-NADIM (d.995), a book-dealer of Baghdad who wrote the famous *Al-Fihrist*, or catalogue, an early comprehensive reference work.

'ALI IBN AHMAD IBN HAZM (d.1064) was a theologian born in Cordova. He opposed the Ash'aris and followed the *Zahiri* (exotericist) School of Law which upheld the explicit meaning of the Qur'an above all other interpretations.

MUHAMMAD IBN HASAN AT-TUSI (d.1067), a Shi'i theologian and author of one of the four basic Shi'i collections of *Hadith*, the *Istibsar* (the 'examination'). He studied under Shaykh al-Mufid and Sayyid Murtadha, and wrote numerous books, including the first catalogue of Shi'i works.

ABU ISMA'IL 'ABD ALLAH AL-ANSARI (d.1089), born near Herat, was a great Sufi master, scholar and theologian. Through his works his spiritual influence continues to this day.

ABU HAMID MUHAMMAD AL-GHAZALI (d.1111) was born and died in Tus in northern Persia. He was a great theologian, jurist, Sufi and reviver of Islam.

'UMAR AL-KHAYYAM (d.1125) was a Persian mathematician and astronomer whose fame rests primarily on his poetical work, the Rub'ayyat.

ABU BAKR MUHAMMAD IBN BAJJAH (d.1138), a philosopher, known in Europe as Avempace, was born in Saragosa, Spain and died in Fez, Morocco. He contributed greatly to making available ancient Greek philosophy and physical science.

ABU'L QASIM MAHMUD IBN 'UMAR AZ-ZAMAKHSHARI (d.1144) was a great Persian authority on the Arabic language, who authored studies on grammar and literature and a famous commentary on the Qur'an.

'ABD AL-QADIR AL-GILANI (d.1166) was one of the great Sufi saints and a descendant of the Prophet. He came from Gilan in north Persia, but lived and died in Baghdad. His teachings and followers are spread throughout the Middle East, the Asian subcontinent, Russia and elsewhere.

SHIHAB AD-DIN YAHYA SUHRAWARDI (d.1191) was the founder of the Ishraqi (illuminationist) school of philosophy in Persia. He was put to death by Saladin on the grounds of heresy.

ABU'L WALID MUHAMMAD IBN AHMAD IBN MUHAMMAD IBN RUSHD (d.1198) was an Arab philosopher of Spain, known to Europe as Averroes through Latin translations of his authoritative work on Aristotelian philosophy. He considered the truth of revealed knowledge to be the higher truth, and theology the lower. His main work harmonized the Qur'an with philosophy and logic. For his pains he was persecuted and exiled more than once between Spain and Morocco.

FARID AD-DIN ATTAR (d.1229) was the Persian Sufi author of *The Language of the Birds*, an allegory of the spiritual path. He also wrote a collection of biographies about prominent Sufis.

IBN AL-FARID (d.1235) was a Sufi master and poet who lived in Egypt and whose enlightening poetry is still popular among seekers.

ABU BAKR MUHAMMAD MUHYI UD-DIN IBN 'ARABI (d.1240), known as the Shaykh Al-Akbar, or the greatest teacher, was born in Murcia but was buried in Damascus. He was possibly the greatest exponent of Islamic metaphysics, and his works, including the monumental *Meccan Revelations* and the *Seals of Wisdom*, are still actively used by serious seekers. There were several women among his teachers, and his teachings were later transmitted by many great saints such as Al-Jili, Imam Shadhili, Rumi and Mulla Sadra.

SHAMS AL-FUQARA (dates unknown) lived in Andalusia at the time of Ibn 'Arabi with whom she had frequent encounters and whom she inspired with her knowledge. She was famous for her piety, ascetic lifestyle and exalted spiritual conduct.

ABU MUHAMMAD 'ABD ALLAH IBN AHMAD DIYA' AD-DIN IBN BAYTAR (d.1248) was a physician, botanist and pharmacist. He was born in Malaga and died in Damascus. His findings were compiled by him into a great and much consulted compendium.

ABU'L HASAN 'ALI IBN 'ABD ALLAH ASH-SHADHILI (d.1258) was born in Tunisia and buried in Egypt. He was the founder of the Shadhiliyyah, one of the most important Sufi brotherhoods in North Africa, and his teachings emphasized *ma'rifah* (gnosis). He was a spiritual descendant of Abu Madyan and Ibn Mashish.

JALAL UD-DIN AR-RUMI (d.1273), born in Balkh, was one of the greatest Persian Sufis. He settled in Konya, Turkey, where he taught religious sciences. He was profoundly influenced by Shams ud-Din Al-Tabrizi, an intoxicated Sufi mystic. His sublime poetical work the *Mathnawi*, a six-volume work of dense spiritual teachings and Sufi lore, has been translated into many languages. The Mevlevi Sufi order (the 'Whirling Dervishes') originate with him.

NASIR AD-DIN AL-TUSI (d.1274), an astronomer, astrologer, mathematician and philosopher, was born in Tus. He is known to have written Isma'ili treatises and other Shi'i books on conduct. He compiled astronomical tables and proposed a model for the study of planetary motion as well as numerous treatises on theosophy and theology.

MUSLAH AD-DIN SA'DI (d.1291), a poet and moralist, hailed from Shiraz, studied at Baghdad and travelled extensively. He was the author of *Bustan* ('The Fruit Garden') and *Gulistan* (The Rose Garden'), and was a disciple of Shihab ad-Din Suhrawardi.

IBN TAYMIYAH (d.1328) grew up in Damascus and became a jurist of the Hanbali School of Law. His literalist interpretation of the Qur'an led him to attack many authorities in Islam, such as Al-Ghazali, Ibn 'Arabi and all Sufis and Shi'is. He is an important forerunner of the Wahhabis.

ABU 'ABD ALLAH MUHAMMAD IBN BATUTA (d.1378) was born in Tangier and travelled extensively throughout Muslim lands as far east as Sumatra. His travelogues vividly describe the cultural and religious life of his times. He is nicknamed the Arab Marco Polo.

NURAD-DIN 'ABD AL-RAHMAN JAMI (1414–1492) was a Persian Sufi poet, famous for his allegorical works such as *Yusuf and Zulaykhah* and *Salman and Absal*.

IMAM SHAMIL (d.1871) was a Naqshbandi Sufi and tribal leader who courageously led the Muslim tribes in Daghestan in their war against the Russian invaders. A strong inspirational figure, he died while on pilgrimage and is buried in Medina.

GLOSSARY

The following is an expanded glossary of the key Arabic terms in this book arranged according to the English alphabet. Transliteration used throughout this book is based on the American Library of Congress system.

Allah God; the Greatest Name of God. Literally 'The God'. Allah designates the Source from which all things seen and unseen emanate and return. The name encompasses all the Divine Names (also known as the Most Beautiful Names of God) such as al-Awwal (the First), al-Akhir (the Last), al-Zahir (the Manifest), al-Batin (the Hidden).

'alim (pl. *'ulama*): a learned man, particularly of Islamic legal and religious studies.

dhikr Remembrance of Allah, stimulated by the invocation of His Divine Names and other formulae from the Qur'an and sayings of the Prophet. From *dhakara*, to remember, think, relate; to strike a man on his private parts. Derivatives: *tadhkirah*, warning, admonition, recollection; *dhakar*, male.

Din Life-transaction. Usually translated as religion which does not transmit the full significance of the term. *Din* is the transaction between the Creditor (Allah) and the indebted (man). From the root *dana*, to owe, be indebted to, take a loan, be inferior. Hence 'living the *din*' means repaying one's debt to the Creator in a manner that befits the high station of man in creation.

fiqh Understanding, comprehension, knowledge. Has come to refer specifically to Islamic jurisprudence; the discipline of elucidating the *Shari'ah*; also the resultant body of rules. A *faqih* (pl. *fuqaha*) is an exponent of *fiqh*. From *faqaha*, to be superior in wisdom, and *faqiha* to be wise, to be skilled in matters pertaining to law; *tafaqqaha* is to be assiduous in instructing oneself.

Hadith Tradition, saying (usually of the Blessed Prophet but sometimes related by the Holy Imams, relating his deeds and utterances); speech, account, narrative. From the verb *hadatha*, to happen, be new; and *haddatha*, to relate or report, speak about.

haqiqah Inner reality, truth, science of the inward; the realm of senses. See also *tariqah* to understand this triad of terms. From *haqqa*, to be true, right, just, authentic, valid; and *haqqaqa*, to realize, make something come true. Divine Name: al-Haqq, the Truth, Whose being is never changed.

iman Faith, trust, belief, acceptance. From *amana*, to believe; and *amina*, to be tranquil in heart and mind, to become safe or secure, to trust; *amana* to render secure, grant safety. *Iman* is being true to the trust with respect to which Allah has confided in one by a firm believing of the heart, not by professing it on the tongue only. Derivatives: *amn*, peace, security, protection (the opposite of *khawf*); *amin*, trustworthy, faithful, honest (designation of the Prophet); *mu'min*, a believer, he who is given certainty and trust; Divine Name: al-Amin, He Who is secure from any causality.

ijma' Agreement of the Muslim community as a ground for legal decisions; what constitutes the community for this purpose is debatable.

ijtihad Individual inquiry to establish the ruling of the *Shari'ah* upon a given point, by a *mujtahid*, a person qualified for the inquiry.

jihad Literally, striving (for the sake of Allah); fighting (so-called Holy War) for the sake of establishing truth and justice in an unbalanced situation. From the verb *jahada*: to endeavour, strive, do one's utmost, expend energy. *Mujahid* is a warrior, fighter.

madhhab (pl. *madhahib*), a system of *fiqh*, or generally the system followed by any given religious group; specifically, four *madhahib*

158

were ultimately accepted as legitimate by the Sunnis, while the Shi'is and *Kharijis* had other *madhahib*. Sometimes rendered 'sect', 'school' or 'rite'.

ma'rifah Gnosis, realization, knowledge on which all knowledge rests. From *'arafa*, to know, recognize, differentiate, perceive. The *'arif*, the gnostic, is he who never sees anything but that he sees Allah in it, before it and after it. In Sufism, *ma'rifah* is part of a triad that includes *makhafah*, 'fear' and *mahabbah* 'love' of God.

mawla (pl. *mawali*), master or servant, also a man of religious authority. In the plural form *mawali* it especially refers to persons associated with Arab tribes other than by birth, particularly in Marwani times; non-Arab converts to Islam.

nafs Self, soul, mind, human being. The *nafs* includes man's innate nature, his genetic predisposition, and his conditioned behaviour. Its manifestation may be base and animalistic, or spiritually elevated, according to the state of its purity. From the verbs *nafusa*, to be precious, valuable; *naffasa*, to comfort, relieve; and *tanaffasa*, to breathe, pause for a rest.

qiyas The principle of deriving new judicial decisions by way of analogy with those given in the body of *Hadith* or the Qur'an. One of the four roots of *fiqh* recognized by Sunnis. From *qasa*, to gauge, measure, compare, correlate.

ribat (pl. *ribatat* and *rubut*), a hospice or fort on the frontier of Islam. From the verb *rabata*, to bind or to post.

riddah Apostasy from Islam. An apostate is a *murtadd*. The word is also applied to the period of insurgency and the rise of false prophets among the desert tribes, which followed the death of the Prophet.

Shari'ah Revealed Islamic code of conduct; the outer path. From the verb *shara'a*, to begin, enter, unbind, introduce, prescribe, give (laws). *Shari'* means road; *mashra'* means spring. It is the complement and container of *haqiqah* for the waters that gush from Reality's spring cannot be contained or drunk from except by a proper vessel.

Sufi An exponent of (*tasawwuf*) Sufism, the commonest term for that aspect of Islam which is based on realizing the seen and unseen.

The Arabic *faqir* and the Persian *darvish*, both meaning 'poor', are applied to Sufis in reference to their poor or wandering life.

Sunnah Way, habitual custom, line of conduct. Used in reference to Allah or the Prophet. From the verb *sanna*, to shape, form, prescribe, enact, establish.

tariqah The Path or way; manner, mode or means. The middle way between *shari'ah* and *haqiqah*. From *taraqa*, to knock, forge, reach. Specifically, any one of the groupings of Sufis with a common chain of transmission and a common invocation. The Prophet said '*Shari'ah* is my words, *tariqah* my acts and *haqiqah* my state'.

waqf (pl. *awqaf*), pious endowment or 'foundation' of certain incomes (commonly rents or land revenues) for the upkeep of a mosque, a hospital, etc. Sometimes the main purpose of such endowment was to provide entailed and unconfiscatable income for one's descendants.

yaqin Certainty. From *yaqina*, to be certain. *Yaqin* has three parts: *'ilm al-yaqin*, the knowledge of certainty; *'ayn al-yaqin*, the source of certainty; and *haqq al-yaqin*, the eye of certainty.

zakat Purity; a portion of one's substance given in order to purify the rest, hence alms tax. From *zakiya*, to grow, be pure or purified.

zawiyah Literally 'corner'. A building for Sufi activities, where *dhikr* was observed and where one or more shaykhs lived, entertained travelling Sufis, and taught their disciples or followers. In Persian it is *khangah*, in Turkish, *tekke*.

BIBLIOGRAPHY

Ali, Syed Ameer – *The Spirit of Islam*, Idarah-i Adabiyat, Delhi, 1922. *A Short History of the Saracens* IBS, Lahore, 1927.

Amine, Hasan ul-, *Shorter Islamic Shi'ite Encyclopedia*, A Group of Muslim Brothers, Beirut, 1969.

Amuli, Hyder, *Inner Secrets of the Path*, transl. by Shaykh Abu 'Ali Fattah, Element Books, Dorset, 1988.

Balagh Foundation, Al-, *Fasting: A Divine Banquet*, Tehran, 1990.

Behisti, Dr M.H. and Bahonar, Dr J., *Philosophy of Islam*, Islamic Seminary, Karachi, 1982.

Brockelman, Carl, *History of Islamic Peoples* RKP, London, 1948.

Chejne, Anwar G. *Muslim Spain: Its History and Culture* U. Minnesota, 1974.

Doi, Abdur Rahman I., *Shariah: The Islamic Law*, Ta Ha, London, 1984.

Dunlop, D.M., *Arab Civilization to AD 1500*, Longman, London, 1971.

Encyclopaedia Brittanica, The New 1989.

Ezzati, A. *The Spread of Islam*, News & Media, London, 1976.

Farah, Caesar E. *Islam: Belief and Observances*, Barrons, New York, 1968.

Ghita, Ayatullah Kashif al-, *The Shia Origin and Faith*, Islamic Seminary, Karachi, 1982.

Gibb, H.A.R., *Islam*, OUP, Oxford, 1949.

Glasse, Cyril, *The Concise Encyclopaedia of Islam*, Stacey, London, 1974.

Guillaume, Alfred, *Islam*, Penguin, London, 1954.

Haeri, Shaykh Fadhlallah, *Man in Qur'an and the Meaning of Furqan*, Zahra, US, 1982.

——*Songs of Iman*, Zahra, US, 1983.

——*Heart of Qur'an and Perfect Mizan*, Zahra, US, 1983.

——*The Mercy of Qur'an and the Advent of Zaman*, Zahra, US, 1984.

——*Beams of Illumination from the Divine Revelation*, Zahra, US, 1985.

——*The Light of Iman from the House of Imran*, Zahra, US, 1986.

——*Journey of the Universe: As Expounded in the Qur'an*, RKP, London, 1985.

——*Beginning's End*, RKP, London, 1987.

——*The Sufi Way to Self Unfoldment*, Element Books, Dorset, 1987.

——*Living Islam East and West*, Element Books, Dorset, 1989.

——*The Journey of the Self*, Element Books, Dorset, 1989.

Harris, Walter, *Morocco That Was*, London, 1983.

Harvey, C.P., *Islamic Spain 1250 to 1500*, London, 1990.

Hassani, Bakir Al, *Language of the Qur'an*, Silver Springs, 1989.

Haykal, M.H., *The Life of Muhammad*, North American Trust, US, 1976.

Hodgson, Marshall G.S., *The Venture of Islam*. Vols. I,II,III, U. Chicago, 1974.

Hourani, Albert, *A History of the Arab Peoples*, Faber, London, 1992.

Husayn, Sayyid Safdar, *The Early History of Islam*, Karachi.

Ibn Al'Arabi, Muhyi 'ddin *The Tarjuman Al-Ashwaq*, Theosophical, 1978.

Ibn Battuta, *Travels in Asia and Africa 1325–1354* Augustus M. Kelly, New York, 1969.

Ibn, Ishaq, *The Life of Muhammad*, transl. by A. Guillaume, OUP, Oxford, 1978.

Islamic Seminary, *Rationality of Islam*, Karachi, 1968.

Lari, Sayyid M.M., *The Seal of the Prophets and His Message*, transl. by Hamid Algar, Islamic Education Center, Qum, 1978.

——*Western Civilization Through Muslim Eyes*, transl. by F.J. Goulding, Tehran, 1977.

Lewis, Bernard, *The Muslim Discovery of Europe*, McLeod, New York, 1982.

——*Islam*, vol. II, Faber, New York, 1974.

Lewis, Raphaela, *Everyday Life in Ottoman Turkey*, Batsford, London, 1971.

Maalouf, Amin, *The Crusaders Through Arab Eyes*, Al Saqi, London 1984.

Majlisi, Allama M. Baqir al-, *The Life and Religion of Muhammad*, vol. II, Zahra, UK, 1982.

Mansel, Philip, *Sultans of Splendour*, BBC, London, 1988.

Mazrui, Ali. A., *The Africans, A Triple Heritage*, BBC, London, 1986.

Meherally, Akbarally, *Understanding the Bible Through Koranic Messages*, AM Trust, Canada, 1989.

Moomen, Majoon, *An Introduction to Shi'i Islam*, Yale University, New York, 1985.

Mottahedeh, Roy, *Mantle of the Prophet: Religion and Politics in Iran*, Princeton, 1986.

Musawi, 'Abd al-Husayn Sharaf al-Din. *The Right Path*, Zahra, US, 1986.

Mutahhari, Murtada, *The Rights of Women in Islam*, WOFIS, Tehran, 1981.

——*Man and Faith*, Iran, 1982.

Muzaffar, Muhammad Rida al-, *The Faith of Shia Islam*, Muhammadi Trust, London, 1982.

Naquib Al-Attas, Seyed M. Al-, *Islam. The Concept of Religion and The Foundation of Ethics and Morality*, RKP, London, 1976.

Naqvi, Ali Muhammad, *A Manual of Islamic Beliefs and Practices*, Muhammadi Trust, London, 1990.

Nasr, Seyyed Hossein, *Muhammad Man of Allah*, Muhammadi Trust, London, 1982.

——*Ideal and Realities of Islam*, George Allen & Unwin, London, 1985.

Nigosian, Solomon, *Islam: The Way of Submission*, Aquarian Press, London, 1987.

Peermahomed Ebrahim Trust, *Selected Judgements of Hazrat Ali*, Karachi.

Qadir As-Sufi, 'Abd Al-, *The Way of Muhammad*, Diwan Press, London, 1975.

Rafi'i, Mustafa Al-, *Islamuna (Our Islam)*, Muhammadi/KPI, London, 1987.

Rahim, Muhammad Ata ur-, *Jesus. A Prophet of Islam*, Taj Company, London, 1987.

Rahman, Afzalur. *Islam. Ideology and the Way of Life*, The Muslim Schools Trust, London, 1980.

Rahnama, Zeinolabedin, *Payambar the Messenger*, vols. I,II,III, transl. by L.P. Elwell-Sutton, Zahra, Bombay, 1982.

Rizvi, S.S. Akhtar, *The Family Life of Islam*, WOFIS, Tehran, 1980.

Sadiq, Imam Ja'far Al-, *The Lantern of the Path*, transl. by Muna Bilgrami, Zahra/Elements Books, Dorset, 1989.

Schuon, Frithjof, *Understanding of Islam*, Unwin Hyman, London, 1976.

Shuster, W. Morgan, *The Strangling of Persia*, New York, 1912.

Smart, Ninian, *The World's Religions*, University of Cambridge, London, 1989.

Stewart, Desmond, *Early Islam*, Time/Life, Netherlands, 1968.

Suhufi, S.M., *Lessons from Islam*, transl. by M.F. Haq, Islamic Seminary, Karachi, 1985.

Tabataba'i, Allamah Sayyid M.H., *The Qur'an in Islam*, Zahra, London, 1987.

——*A Shi'ite Anthology*, transl. by William C. Chitick, Muhammadi Trust, London, 1980.

Thomson, Ahmed, *Blood on the Cross*, Ta Ha Publ., London, 1989.

INDEX

165